BY WILLIAM D. COHAN

Why Wall Street Matters

The Price of Silence: The Duke Lacrosse Scandal, the Power of the Elite, and the Corruption of Our Great Universities

Money and Power: How Goldman Sachs Came to Rule the World

House of Cards: A Tale of Hubris and Wretched Excess on Wall Street

The Last Tycoons: The Secret History of Lazard Frères & Co.

WHY
WALL STREET
MATTERS

WHY WALL STREET MATTERS

William D. Cohan

RANDOM HOUSE

NEW YORK

ISBN 978-0-399-59069-6
Ebook ISBN 978-0-399-59070-2

Printed in the United States of America on acid-free paper

randomhousebooks.com

2 4 6 8 9 7 5 3 1

First Edition

Book design by Caroline Cunningham

To Teddy, Quentin, and Deb

CONTENTS

INTRODUCTION

What Is Wall Street?

The conversation we've been having about Wall Street in this country for the past decade has become so utterly hyperbolic, supercharged, entrenched, and polemic that if you're like most people, amid all the outrage you've totally lost the thread of the discussion. Maybe you think the whole system is rotten to the core. Maybe you think, sure, there's greed, excess, and bad behavior on Wall Street, with nary a consequence for those responsible, but is the right answer to these problems to break up the big banks? Maybe that's about when you just checked out.

Even the phrase "Wall Street" conjures confusion. What are we talking about? The actual place? Just the very biggest investment banks, or the smaller ones, too? Does the term include hedge funds and private-equity firms?

Are we talking about the entire New York finance community? Do we include the banks, hedge funds, and private-equity firms in the rest of the country? What about the financial system of the entire globe? What are we even referring to anymore? Most people haven't a clue. William Faulkner once described the American South as less of a "geographical place" than an "emotional idea." Is Wall Street simply an emotional idea?

The questions keep piling up. Maybe we can define what we mean by Wall Street, but even if we do, how should we *feel* about it? Should we be angry that Wall Street seems to be nothing more than a festering, open wound of rampant self-interest and malfeasance? Or should we be happy that Wall Street has become a convenient metaphor that politicians use to park blame for every bad economic thing that has befallen the country in recent years?

Or could it be that Wall Street is something altogether very different? Is Wall Street the left ventricle of capitalism, the brilliantly designed engine that powers innovation, job growth, and wealth creation and that has become the most sustained way by which billions of people the world over have been lifted out of poverty and given a chance at a better, more economically fulfilling life?

Is Wall Street a cause for celebration or denigration?

This is a fundamental question that has become so

charged and shouted over that by now most people don't know how to answer it. Or don't dare to try. But if they are pressed, their instinct would likely be to agree with Jean-Jacques Rousseau, the eighteenth-century Enlightenment philosopher, who once said that "finance" is "a slave's word," while the profession itself is nothing more than "a means of making pilferers and traitors, and of putting freedom and the public good upon the auction block." The modern-day equivalent of this sentiment can be found in the musings of Bernie Sanders, the U.S. senator from Vermont and former Democratic presidential candidate, whose stump speeches during the 2016 presidential campaign condemned Wall Street relentlessly. "Greed, fraud, dishonesty and arrogance, these are the words that best describe the reality of Wall Street today," he said in January 2016. And then he paid homage to one of the most recognizable cultural touchstones about modern Wall Street when he referred to the famous "Greed is good" scene in *Wall Street*, the 1987 Oliver Stone film, where Gordon Gekko, played with oleaginous glee by Michael Douglas, lectures Bud Fox, his young and aspiring apprentice (played by Charlie Sheen). "So, to those on Wall Street who may be listening today, let me be very clear," Senator Sanders continued. "Greed is not good. In fact, the greed of Wall Street and corporate America is destroying the fabric of our nation . . . We will no longer tolerate an economy and a political system that has been rigged by Wall Street to benefit the wealthiest Americans in this country at the expense of everyone else."

Senator Sanders used his growing political power to influence the anti–Wall Street rhetoric of the Democratic Party's 2016 platform. "To restore economic fairness," the platform reads, "Wall Street cannot be an island unto itself, gambling trillions in risky financial instruments and making huge profits, all the while thinking that taxpayers will be there to bail them out again. We must tackle dangerous risks in big banks and elsewhere in the financial system." And to do this, the Democrats advocated "breaking up too-big-to-fail financial institutions that pose a systemic risk to the stability of our economy" and an "updated and modernized" version of the so-called Glass-Steagall Act of 1933, which forced the separation of investment banking from commercial banking for the next sixty-six years, until its repeal in 1999. Plugging his new book, *Our Revolution: A Future to Believe In,* after the election of Donald Trump, Senator Sanders continues to lambast Wall Street. Hell, Wall Street has grown so unpopular that even the 2016 *Republican* Party platform called for the reinstatement of Glass-Steagall. Just think about *that* for a moment. Rest assured, Trump's victory does not necessarily mean that the populist anger directed toward Wall Street dissolves overnight.

So, is Senator Sanders correct? Is Wall Street actually rigged to benefit the rich in America at the expense of everyone else? Or is what Wall Street does in its many guises—and as we can see by all the questions just asked, there are a variety of different aspects to what gets lumped together as "Wall Street" these days—a monumentally important, utterly irreplaceable way that capital gets allocated in the most efficient, fairly priced manner from the people who have it to the people who want it?

How can it be, as the British economist, money manager, and writer Felix Martin observed, that high finance is "at one and the same time something so completely mysterious and so utterly banal"? To be sure, there are many crucial challenges facing the world today—among them climate change, income inequality, suppression of human rights, nuclear proliferation, and political unrest—but our collective failure to decide whether Wall Street is a force for good or one for evil, whether it should be celebrated or dismantled, certainly ranks high among them and effectively precludes us from having a much-needed debate about what Wall Street does right, and should be encouraged, and what Wall Street does wrong, and should be eliminated.

This, then, is my effort to pry open the black box that Wall Street has carefully constructed around itself in the last generation, much to its detriment. It's a black box that makes it almost impossible for the average American to understand what goes on there, why it is important to nearly everything we hold dear, and why we wouldn't much like to live in a world without Wall Street. True, Wall Street does itself no favors by constantly using its own confusing, specialized jargon. People get rightfully befuddled by most of the words used by Wall Street bankers, traders, and executives. Take, for instance, the word "securities," which is nothing more than Wall Street argot for an ownership position in a stock—the equity value of a corporation—or a bond, which is a creditor's right to receive fixed payments (plus the return of the principal) from a corporation, or a government entity, over time in exchange for lending money to it. If you're like most people, though, once you hear the term "leveraged buyout" or "credit default swap," your eyes glaze over and you mentally check out. Or maybe you are just utterly confused by the fact that after attacking Wall Street mercilessly during his campaign, Donald Trump has surrounded himself with Wall Street veterans.

But here's the thing: If you like your iPhone (which you clearly do, because more than one billion iPhones have been sold worldwide since its inception in June

2007), or your wide-screen TV, or your car, or your morning bacon, or your pension, or your 401(k), then you are a fan of Wall Street, whether you know it or not. If you like the power and functionality of Facebook, Snapchat, and Twitter, you actually like Wall Street. None of these things would be even remotely possible to have, in the size and the scope that we have them, and as affordable and as easily accessible as they are, without the free flow of capital that Wall Street manages to provide nearly twenty-four hours a day, seven days a week to people who need it anywhere on the globe. The ability of Wall Street to provide capital when and where it is needed at a fair price isn't a magic trick, or a strange form of alchemy, or something to be feared, or detested. It is an essential fact of modern-day life.

It should be celebrated.

At the same time, of course, Wall Street is a business, a big business. Everything it does is designed to make money, or is done with the hope of making money, just like any other business on Earth. It doesn't deserve or warrant extra vilification as a result. For instance, it's no surprise that Apple would not exist if it weren't profitable, or weren't able to convince investors that one day it would be (as companies such as Amazon have been able to do for years). The fact that Apple is one of the most profitable companies in the world enables it to hire the best, the brightest, and the most creative people and pay them well. Apple's success allows it to buy new equipment and to build new plants—including a space-age, $5 billion circular headquarters in Cupertino, California—and, of course, it allows Apple to design and to build new groundbreaking products, such as the iPod, the iPhone, and the Apple Watch, and to dream about what the future will look like, whether it includes the Apple car or the Apple personal transporter, like *The Jetsons*.

I know that in the current political climate, that might sound like a heavy dose of corporate pabulum, courtesy of a Wall Street or Apple flack, but here's the point: It's absolutely, demonstrably true. Companies like Apple need Wall Street to achieve their destiny and to become great.

Admittedly, Apple's products are first-world luxuries. But their appeal goes well beyond the pockets of rich Westerners. People all over the world, from nearly every walk of life, either own Apple products or aspire to own them. And for good reason: The amount of computing power in an iPhone, which can be carried in a pocket, is unprecedented in human history, as is the amount of information that can be accessed from it. That doesn't mean it's not fair to ask whether gold miners in Africa or factory workers in China are being exploited for the benefit of Apple's shareholders, management, and customers. Or to continue to ask what must be done to help the more than 1.3 billion people worldwide who live in extreme poverty. But Apple's success is extraordinary. It has created nearly 700,000 jobs worldwide that are tied to either Apple or its ecosystem. It has created products that many people love and *need*. Say what you will, the iPhone is an amazing piece of technology that has changed the world. That is a good thing. It is how the human race advances. It rightly deserves the praise it has garnered.

Here's the part Bernie would hate but be unable to disprove: Very little of Apple's success story—it is the world's most valuable company—could have been written without Wall Street. Even a quick perusal of Apple's IPO prospectus—the document that is required to be filed with the Securities and Exchange Commission (SEC) before a company's stock, the value of a company after its debt and other obligations are satisfied, can be sold to the public and then traded—reveals the essential role that Wall Street played, and still plays, in figuring out, at each step of the way, how Apple—as well as millions of other companies around the world that want to be like Apple—gets the money it needs to operate and to achieve its dreams. This is not trivial. It is not unimportant. It is not evil. Nor is it meant to be mysterious. But very few people understand just how this happens or why it is essential. Instead, if they think about it at all, they probably see Wall Street bankers taking large fees for what seems like minimal risk (although there is certainly more risk than meets the eye). They chalk it up to "greedy bankers" and a "rigged" system and move on.

But the ongoing ability of companies to get the capital they need from the people who have it and want to invest it is one of the more amazing contraptions that the world has ever constructed. It's not the least bit clear what the world would be like without Wall Street. (Perhaps it would look more like the Middle Ages?) And that's why it's essential that the American people understand better what makes Wall Street tick, what it does right, and what it does wrong.

Let's back up for a minute. The December 1980 Apple IPO prospectus distills down generations of Wall Street art and science into a crisp forty-seven pages. Nearly everything an investor would want to know about Apple is included: how and when the company was formed; how it was financed and by whom; who owned the pre-IPO stock; and how Apple intended to use the proceeds from the IPO. That's not a coincidence. In fact, it is government regulation at its best. One of the main reasons the Securities and Exchange Commission was created in the wake of the stock market crash of 1929 was to provide investors, or potential investors, with more information about the companies that wanted their money and to try to thwart charlatans. The Apple prospectus resulted from regulators at the SEC making sure that Apple complied with disclosure rules in ways that were not required before the creation of the SEC. This is a good thing.

Objectively speaking, we learn from the Apple prospectus that there would be no Apple, at least in its present form, without Wall Street. The prospectus explains that Apple had a relatively large group of early investors who supported the company from its inception in 1976, when Steve Jobs and Steve Wozniak, the two founders, "designed, developed and assembled the Apple I, a microprocessor-based computer consisting of a single printed circuit board." On January 3, 1977, Apple incorporated; three months later, it introduced the Apple II, which was similar to the Apple I but with a keyboard and a plastic cover. For the nine months leading up to the end of September 1977, Apple had a profit of almost $45,000.

But Apple had big ambitions, as the prospectus makes clear, and achieving those ambitions required capital. Lots of it. That capital came from many sources at various times. Most important, at first, were the venture capitalists, such as Venrock Associates, in New York City, which had a 7.6 percent stake in Apple at the time of its IPO, and Arthur Rock, a former banker at Hambrecht & Quist, a small technology-oriented investment bank in San Francisco. Rock had a 1.3 percent stake in Apple. There were other venture capitalists, too, and together they owned another 8.7 percent of Apple before its IPO. As for Jobs, then twenty-five years old, and Wozniak, then thirty years old, they had stakes in Apple of 15 percent and 7.9 percent, respectively. A. C. Markkula Jr., Apple's chief marketing executive since May 1977 and also the chairman of the board of directors, had a 14 percent stake. Michael Scott, Apple's short-lived first CEO, bought his stake of nearly 1.3 million shares for a penny a share when he joined Apple in May 1977.

The venture capitalists backing Apple did so for one reason: They were hoping to make money. Some believed they would get rich. The thought process that led Venrock and Arthur Rock to invest in Apple is the same one that leads to any investment being made, even ones in Wall Street firms. That's the way capitalism tends to work: Investors are willing to take exceptional risks—and backing Apple financially in 1977 was an exceptional risk because it was all big dreams and little accomplishment—in the hope of achieving an exceptional return on that investment. And the Apple IPO certainly made the earliest investors in Apple wealthy. Many of them paid less than ten cents a share for their stock. Considering that the IPO was priced at $22 per share, the return on that initial investment was astounding. (Had these investors held on until the present day, the wealth creation would have been nearly beyond comprehension. Indeed, Laurene

Powell Jobs, the widow of Steve Jobs, is said to be worth around $19 billion.) Of course, it doesn't always work out the way the Apple IPO did. The landscape is strewn with corporate carcasses and with investors who bet wrong and lost. But betting wrong and losing is as important to the success of capitalism as is making a smart investment and making a fortune.

The Apple IPO prospectus also revealed other ways, along with providing venture capital, that Wall Street helped the company achieve its early goals. As many companies do, Apple had arranged for a $20 million line of credit with a bank. Apple paid interest on its bank borrowings, based on the prime rate, which in September 1980 was 12 percent. The bank made the loan to Apple for one reason only: It wanted to make money. Apple also had $2 million of capital leases that allowed it to finance the purchase of various manufacturing and office facilities as well as automobiles. Apple paid interest on the leases to a bank, which made the money available to Apple for one reason: to make money on the money it lent Apple.

Underwriting the Apple IPO itself was another way for Wall Street to make money; an IPO is one of the most profitable products that Wall Street sells its corporate customers, charging fees generally of around 7 percent of the money raised to cover the risk of buying the stock from a company, finding new investors, and then immediately selling the company's stock to them. The Apple IPO, in December 1980, raised $102 million, of which some $83 million went to Apple, $12.4 million went to the venture capitalists who sold shares in the IPO, and the remaining $6 million went to the underwriters, led by Morgan Stanley and Hambrecht & Quist, as fees for their trouble. (In this case, Jobs negotiated the fee down to 6 percent from 7 percent.) The Apple IPO was "hot," meaning that both underwriters and investors wanted into the deal. Indeed, the sheer number of Wall Street banks involved in underwriting the deal was extraordinary: The prospectus lists nearly 140 banks from around the world that participated by selling stock to investors. Many of those underwriters—such as Barings Bank, Bear Stearns, and Lehman Brothers—are long gone, which shows that contrary to what you might think, Wall Street has always been a dangerous and risky place. And risks do have consequences, even for Wall Street.

The $83 million that Wall Street delivered to Apple was far more money than the company had ever raised in its four-year existence. For that reason alone, the IPO would have been considered a success. And Apple had plenty of uses for the money it raised: $7.85 million was used to repay its outstanding bank loan, and the rest of the money allowed Apple, essentially, to act as its own bank in financing its working capital needs. Apple also intended to use $11 million of the proceeds to fund big new projects in 1981. It said it did not anticipate making further borrowings but also alerted its new equity investors that it might do so in the future. By any measure, the Apple IPO was an unqualified success: for the company, for the new investors, for the selling shareholders, and for the Wall Street banks that underwrote the deal.

I am not arguing that Wall Street is above reproach—far from it—but I am saying that the essential elements of Wall Street—Wall Street in its purest and most practical forms—must be preserved, encouraged, and praised, while the behavior that has caused one financial crisis after another in the past thirty years—rewarding bankers, traders, and executives with millions of dollars in bonuses for taking risks with other people's money without any accountability—must be stopped. Consider this a plea for a calm, thoughtful examination of how Wall Street evolved from a handful of traders on a cobblestoned street that once connected the East River to the Hudson River in lower Manhattan to the global financial behemoth that exists today, with its metaphorical fingers in trillions of dollars of annual transactions.

Wall Street is the capital in capitalism, and even when

we hate its greed and recklessness, we not only *need* Wall Street to exist but *want* it to *thrive,* even when we think, or are led to believe, that we don't.

You can't legislate away human nature. Human beings have a knack for ruthless competition and for seeking unfair advantages. Reprehensible human behavior has always been around. So let's face it: *There have been financial crises long before there even was a Wall Street.*

That's something we rarely get told: Wall Street is generally not the cause of financial crises; rather, it is the place a financial crisis often first expresses itself. In any event, financial crises are nothing new, and we do ourselves no favors by acting as if they were. For instance, in 1636 and early 1637, in Holland, there was the "mania" related to Dutch tulip bulbs, which sent the price of the bulbs soaring to ridiculous levels before the price collapsed in February 1637. In 1720, there were two bubbles in two European countries, both of which ended very badly: the South Sea Bubble, in Britain, which was the ill-fated idea where the British government granted the South Sea Company exclusive trading rights with South American countries in exchange for the South Sea Company's refinancing Britain's war debt; and the Mississippi Bubble, in France, a strange scheme by a Scottish economist, John Law, to try to compensate a frustrated French populace with the shares of a company that had been created to try to exploit the supposed riches of the land that France owned in the Mississippi River valley, known as Louisiana. In the end, there was nothing to be found—at that time—in Louisiana, although there was plenty of speculation about what might have been there and whether the French government would back the investments up with gold or with paper money.

There was, of course, no Wall Street when these financial crises occurred.

Remembering the past is important because the American people have been poor stewards of the details of their collective financial history. We have little recollection of previous financial crises and seem to relish treating each new one as a revelation—as if it never could have or should have happened at all. As a result, a rational debate—about the causes of a financial crisis, how best to resolve it, and how to create effective policies, regulations, and incentives to try to stave off the inevitable next one—has become nearly impossible to have. Instead, the people with the loudest megaphones—those like Senators Sanders and Elizabeth Warren—who dominate the airwaves on the topic of Wall Street's evils and what to do to curb them, seem to have the least knowledge about the way Wall Street really works and to be especially ignorant about what a world without Wall Street would be like. (Of course, Senator Warren doesn't seem to be complaining about the $1.6 million advance she received for her 2014 book, *A Fighting Chance*, which, I might add, was only remotely possible thanks in large part to the fact that Wall Street provides the financing to the publishing house that bought her book.)

The truth is that I agree with much of the progressive agendas advocated by Senators Sanders and Warren and I have voted Democratic my entire adult life. But they haven't a clue when it comes to understanding Wall Street. They, and the very people who call for breaking up the banks, wouldn't want to live in the world *without* those very banks, even if their rhetoric implies that they would. Nor would the people they claim to speak for— millions of middle-class and working-class Americans— want to live in that world, either. And if our most powerful elected leaders are woefully undereducated about the importance of Wall Street and the role that it plays in keeping our economy humming, well, then it's not the least bit surprising that the American people have virtually no clue about how Wall Street works, either.

This book is an attempt to prove to you why you, as an American, should want Wall Street to exist and to succeed. It is also meant to serve as a starting point for a long-overdue, nonhysterical national debate about how to retain the best of Wall Street while eliminating the incentives that tend to foster the basest instincts of human nature and that lead Wall Street bankers, traders, and executives to misbehave on a regular basis. The goal is to continue to improve the quality of life for Americans—for everybody, really.

The challenge is not to try to prevent another financial crisis from ever happening, as seems to be the new mantra of the most powerful Washington regulators: There will be another financial crisis somewhere at some point whether you obliterate Wall Street or not. Rather, the overarching necessity is to regulate Wall Street in such a way that preserves the things that it does right while also making sure that the people who work there have the correct incentives to *not* do the things that lead to financial calamities, the pain of which seems to be unfairly felt most acutely by the rest of us. More specifically, it is the responsibility of the Justice Department to hold Wall Street bankers, traders, and executives responsible for their questionable, and sometimes criminal, behavior. Just because in the wake of the 2008 financial crisis the Justice Department, under the former attorney general Eric Holder, failed miserably in that important role doesn't mean that Washington's politicians and the powerful Wall Street regulators should therefore adopt policies that sharply curtail the great things Wall Street has done for centuries. That's the kind of thinking that not only penalizes Wall Street but also hurts the rest of us.

I know history can bore people, but sometimes you have to understand at least the basics of how something developed in order to have any grasp of it at all. So let's go very quickly through how Wall Street came to be.

WHY
WALL STREET
MATTERS

CHAPTER 1

The Beginning

The actual Wall Street, in downtown Manhattan, near the island's southern tip, is just seven-tenths of a mile long and runs from Broadway and Trinity Church to the west and to South Street to the east. It used to be the thoroughfare that connected the East River to the Hudson. (The interstitial role played by Wall Street remains as essential as ever.) Wall Street was named after an actual wall—composed of twelve-foot-high wooden logs—that the Dutch inhabitants started building in April 1653, with the help of African slaves, as the northern border of their relatively small enclave. North of the wall was danger and hilly wilderness—the name Manhattan derives from *Mannahatta,* the Lenape Indian term for "island of hills." The Dutch built the wall to protect themselves

3

from the unknown. Indeed, years of fighting between the Dutch and various Native American tribes would be devastating to both sides. The "palisades," as the Dutch referred to the wall, separated what is today Wall Street from everything else to its north. It was 2,340 feet long, nearly half a mile. But by 1664, the Dutch had run out of gas in New Amsterdam and turned their colony over to the British, who promptly renamed it New York.

In 1685, the British surveyors designed a street to run the length of the wall, from the East River to the Hudson, and by 1699 the British—now less fearful of the Native Americans than the Dutch had been—ordered the actual wall removed, leaving only a thoroughfare that stretched from one side of the island to the other, at one of its particularly narrow parts.

The new street—now known as Wall Street—became New York's central artery of commerce. "Few streets in the world are entitled to equal fame," Frederick Trevor Hill wrote in his 1908 gem, *The Story of a Street*. "In the annals of American history, it holds a place apart." Small merchants established themselves along the street to sell their wares, and over time this came to include the sale of stocks and bonds, a form of borrowed money that was still a new concept at the time, of fledgling local companies. Also for sale on Wall Street were slaves. According to the New-York Historical Society, the slave trade in New Amsterdam began in the 1620s—1626 to be exact, less than two years after the Dutch landed in New Amsterdam—after a Dutch ship captured a Spanish or Portuguese vessel, with a largely African crew. Often the crews of captured ships were killed, but in this instance the Dutch brought the crew to New Amsterdam, where it was placed in servitude to the Dutch West India Company.

The company's calculus was a simple and cruel one, alas. It needed laborers to build out the colony of New Amsterdam, to build the fort that is now Battery Park, to build homes, and to build the wall that became Wall Street. But New Amsterdam was not a particularly hospitable place to live, and so attracting Dutch workers to cross the Atlantic was not so easy. The better way, it seemed, to get the labor the Dutch West India Company needed was to enslave it. Charitably, the New-York Historical Society described the Dutch's enslavement of Africans as New Amsterdam's first public works department. "They cut the road that became Broadway," it explained. "They built the wall for which Wall Street is named. Without their work, the colony of New Amsterdam might not have survived."

Soon enough, individual colonists owned slaves. In

fact, according to the historical society, the colony became the largest "slave-holding city" in the northern
colonies.

For fifty-one years, between 1711 and 1762, Wall Street
housed the colony's well-established slave market, in a
wooden shed, hard on the East River, allowing for immediate trading once boats carrying the people from Africa
or the Caribbean tied up at the docks. At any one time,
fifty slaves could be found being bought and sold in the
structure. The sordid practice was ended in 1762 and the
shed eventually torn down, apparently because the structure was blocking views to the river and lowering property values.

Wall Street housed the colony's more noble aspira-
tions as well. In 1699, stones removed from the footings
of the original wall were used for the foundation of what
became, a year later, New York's first City Hall, at 26 Wall
Street. Not surprisingly, City Hall, built at a cost of more
than £4,000, was at the heart of Wall Street. In it, there
was a courtroom, a jury room, the Common Council
chamber, a jail, a library—the first in New York, consisting of 1,642 books that had once been the collection of
the Reverend John Millington—a debtors' prison, and
the offices of the fire department, whose water was supplied from two wells, also dug on Wall Street. Directly
across from City Hall, on Broad Street, lay the stockade,

meant to be a living, breathing symbol to the colonists of the fate that awaited bad behavior.

In short order, as incredible as this may seem today, Wall Street also became a center of revolutionary fervor. It's where the copies of John Peter Zenger's *New-York Weekly Journal*—in which Zenger criticized the royal governor—were burned by the colonial masters and where, on August 4, 1735, inside the City Hall courthouse, Zenger won a resounding legal victory for freedom of the press that has since been dubbed "the dawn of American liberty." Wall Street was where, in 1765, the so-called Stamp Act Congress convened to vigorously—and successfully—oppose the British imposition of a stamp tax on New Yorkers. It was where Paul Revere arrived in May 1774 to announce the first stirrings of the American Revolution.

But in the years after the Revolutionary War, Philadelphia, rather than New York, was the locus of the nation's financial power. New York was a mess, having suffered mightily during the war itself. It was in Philadelphia, not New York, that Robert Morris, the financier and great friend of George Washington's, sought to create the first private, commercial bank in the United States, in the vein of those that had been in existence for centuries in Europe. Following a detailed proposal to the Continental Congress for the bank on May 17, 1781, the Congress chartered it nine days later. Within weeks, Morris was sending letters to potential investors, in effect creating the country's first IPO, or initial public offering, of stock. In a letter on June 11 to the likes of Thomas Jefferson, then governor of Virginia, and John Hancock, then governor of Massachusetts, Morris made his case. He saw it as his duty to create the bank as a way of restoring the financial reputation of the new republic, which had been incurring debts to pay for its revolutionary war but could not afford to repay them. He promised a desirable rate of return on any investment in the stock of the bank. He said investors would feel both pride and patriotism and that the bank would last as long as the United States. (The remnants of Morris's first bank are now part of Wells Fargo.)

The bank began operating the following January after its successful IPO, and its investors believed the stock would become more valuable over time as the bank did more and more profitable business. Eight years later, in 1790, Philadelphia, by then the most populous and prosperous city in the country, created the nation's first stock exchange, some two years before New York embarked on its own version. At about the same time, Alexander Hamilton proposed to Congress that a second bank—the Bank of the United States—be established in Philadelphia. And in 1791, Hamilton succeeded, also through an IPO, in creating the bank, with the U.S. government buying 20 percent of the bank's stock using a loan from the bank itself. Soon enough, brokers and merchants along the Eastern Seaboard of the United States were buying and selling the stock of the two Philadelphia banks.

By then, the practice was nearly two centuries old. The first modern IPO occurred in 1604, with the public sale of stock of the Dutch East India Company, to which a monopoly had been given to harvest the riches of the faraway Spice Islands: nutmeg, cloves, cinnamon, pepper, and ginger. No different than we do today, the founders of the company wanted to raise capital from investors to finance its business—the building and the sending of ships on the long voyage to the other side of the world to obtain the spices it would sell to its customers. The IPO was a watershed moment in the history of capitalism: It proved that capital could be raised from people having nothing to do with the founding or management of a company and that investors would be willing to take what they hoped would be prudent risks in exchange for an expected return. It's an idea that changed the world and remains as vibrant today as it was more than four hundred years ago. At the same time, the Amsterdam Stock Exchange was created to allow for the trading of the East India Company's stock. For more than one hundred years, East India's stock performed well—at one point in 1720, it was trading for twelve times its IPO price—until New Year's Eve 1799, when the company was suddenly dissolved after nearly two hundred years, an important reminder that investing in a company's equity has always been a risky proposition and that even a corporate lifetime of nearly two centuries is no guarantee of survival.

Despite being trumped by Philadelphia for years as the nation's financial center, Wall Street was slowly recovering from the Revolutionary War. The first so-called golden age of Wall Street lasted for seven years in the 1780s, during which brief time New York City was the capital of the young republic, the center of its nascent political and financial might. The first Congress of the United States was built and convened on Wall Street. George Washington was inaugurated as the nation's first president on Wall Street in 1789 and John Adams, its first vice president. During this era, Wall Street was completely rebuilt—including both the Trinity Church and the First Presbyterian Church—and many fine homes and taverns lined the road. It attracted the likes of Alexander Hamilton and Aaron Burr, both young attorneys with thriving legal practices. In June 1784, before moving to Philadelphia and starting his second bank, Hamilton created the Bank of New York, with $500,000 in capital. He wrote its constitution and became one of its first directors. Wall Street was also where Hamilton drafted the essays that would form the majority of what became known as the Federalist Papers, the veritable intellectual blueprint of the new nation. It was where President Washington, on September 24, 1789, signed the law creating the Supreme Court of the United States, including the New Yorker John Jay among the first justices. Between 1783 and 1790, Wall Street might as well have been the center of the universe.

That began to change again in January 1790, when Hamilton, the first Treasury secretary, proposed a complex financial plan by which the federal government would absorb the debt of the states—amounting to roughly $54 million in Hamilton's accounting, including both foreign and domestic obligations—that had accumulated during the War of Independence, in part because the Continental Congress had pushed its debts to the states.

Hamilton's solution, in simple terms, was to have the federal government take over the entirety of the obligations, including both principal and interest, and then to, in effect, tax the states to help to service the new federal debt that would be issued to replace the existing state debt. The plan upset many citizens in the individual states, especially those in places such as Virginia, which had better managed its war debts but would now have to jointly help cover the federal debt. Hamilton also was heavily criticized for paying off the war debt at a hundred cents on the dollar, even though much of it was in the hands of speculators, who had bought the debt at a discount as it became increasingly clear that the new government might not be able to pay it back. Many saw Hamilton's plan as a way to reward speculators, much like how, 218 years later, many would criticize the federal government's bailouts of failing Wall Street banks and of AIG, the insurance behemoth.

Indeed the outrage over Hamilton's proposal was so intense that a compromise had to be fashioned. As the musical *Hamilton* reminds us, a deal was cut over dinner at the New York City home of Thomas Jefferson, by then secretary of state. "So bitter was the feeling against the Federal plan that Hamilton was forced to offer great concessions to carry his point, and the compromise he negotiated disposed of New York as the permanent national capital," Frederick Hill wrote. What Jefferson and Hamilton had concocted, in order to win approval for Hamilton's government bailout of the languishing war debt, was for the capital of the United States to be moved to the banks of the Potomac River. As part of the compromise, for ten years while the new capital was being built, Philadelphia would serve as the nation's capital. And all because Hamilton believed that the United States would not be able to flourish as a deadbeat nation. He was right.

On July 16, 1790, on Wall Street, President Washington

signed the bill into law. He would never return to New York City. In short order, brokers convened in Philadelphia, where the first federal bond—for $80 million—was sold to investors in order to refinance the debt from the Revolutionary War. Traders in New York quickly bought, sold, and traded the bonds, marking another important milestone in the history of finance: the opportunity for an investor to sell a security to a broker, or middleman, when he or she needed to or wanted to. The middlemen were willing to take the risk of buying a bond from a seller until a new buyer of it could be found. Of course, they were hoping to do so at a profit—selling the bond for more than they bought it for—but that was not, *is not*, always possible, introducing a new layer of risk into the business of Wall Street.

With its importance in national politics much diminished, Wall Street collectively set about remaking itself into the nation's center of finance. The United States became one of the few countries in the world to have its seat of political power in a different place from its center of financial power. The city's first "stock exchange" was opened at 22 Wall Street on March 1, 1792, by a group of "auctioneers" who had been designated by the Treasury to sell the bonds that were issued in order to pay off the young nation's debt in accordance with Hamilton's plan. Farther east on Wall Street, at around 70 Wall Street, stood one of the lone trees—a buttonwood tree, which we now call a sycamore—that had survived the Revolutionary War intact and thus had metaphorical importance to the young nation. Under that tree, a small group of brokers had already been in the business of buying and selling the new nation's Treasury debt. They had also been meeting and trading at the Tontine Coffee House, farther east on Wall Street, which was named after a seventeenth-century method of raising capital devised by Lorenzo de Tonti, an Italian, and which was particularly popular in France. The traders were not pleased that the Treasury had appointed the "auctioneers" its exclusive agents.

On May 17, 1792, in an effort to break up the power of the "monopolist" auctioneers farther west on Wall Street, a group of two dozen brokers and merchants entered into what became known as the Buttonwood Agreement, the earliest known written codification of how securities brokers—people who buy and sell stocks and bonds—would work together. The twenty-four brokers "do hereby solemnly promise and pledge ourselves to each other, that we will not buy or sell from this day for any person whatsoever, any kind of Public Stock, at a less rate than one quarter percent Commission on the Specie value and that we will give preference to each other in our Negotiations," according to the agreement. Hamilton's Bank of New York became the first stock traded on the new exchange. By 1798, it was headquartered at what is now 48 Wall Street. Over time, the brokers succeeded in breaking the cartel of the "monopolists," and the NYSE became one of the places where stocks and bonds could be bought and sold—in effect creating a fair market for capital, another hugely important step in the development of the process whereby capital flows from the people who have it and want to invest to the people who need it to start or to grow businesses.

For almost as long as it has been in existence, despite its being the most important financial achievement the world has ever produced, Wall Street has often played the role as the nation's designated villain. The animosity directed at Wall Street today dates back centuries.

In fact, in 1887, Henry Clews, a British-born American financier whose eponymous firm was a leading underwriter of the federal bonds used to pay for the Civil War, picked up his pen and used it to defend his profession from a seemingly endless barrage of criticism then directed at Wall Street. He was tired of the popular depiction of financiers as craven, greedy egoists. "It seems to be a genial pastime for men in various walks of life who know very little about financial affairs, and the methods of doing business in Wall [S]treet, to denounce this great centre of the moneyed interests, as the sum of all villain-ies, a kind of Pandora's box, but without any hope at the bottom," he wrote. Instead, he argued, Wall Street is "a great civilizer, and the mighty channel through which has flown the enormous wealth that has been powerful and necessary in developing our industrial enterprises" and that rather than worthy of denigration Wall Street men, "generally, are paragons of personal honor"—and here referring to their role in financing the Civil War—"and that they were chiefly instrumental in providing the means of saving the nation in the hour of its peril."

Clews conceded that once the nation's best and bright-est would have been ashamed to be seen on Wall Street, let alone work there, but that was no longer true. "Now, men in the same sphere are proud of the distinction, both so-cially and financially," he continued. "In fact, Wall [S]treet has become a necessity, and a healthy stimulant to the rest of the business of the country. Everything looks to this centre as an index of its prosperity. It moves the money that controls the affairs of the world." *It moves the money that controls the affairs of the world.* As true in 2017 as it was in 1887, and before, except now the amount of money flowing through Wall Street on a regular basis is in the *trillions* of dollars.

He believed that Wall Street should be applauded for its service to the nation, not denigrated. "Wall Street has furnished the money that has set the wheels of industry in motion over the vast continent, and in one century has brought us abreast, in the industrial arts, of countries that had from one to two thousand years the start of us," he wrote.

Clews was no naïf. He knew that some of his brethren were bound for bad behavior—although mostly he blamed outsiders to the industry, rather than those who had grown up in it and had been properly trained—and that too often the American people would suffer as a result. "It is true the honor of Wall Street is sometimes slightly tarnished, especially in the eyes of those who reside at a great distance, owing to the occasional delinquencies of dishonorable men, who consider Wall Street men and Wall Street money fair game for swindling operations," he wrote. "These are for the most part outsiders, who pounce upon the Street as their illegitimate prey, after probably making a show of doing business there. There is no place, of course, where confidence men have the opportunity of reaping such a rich harvest when they can succeed in establishing the confidential relations that help them to secure their swag. But Wall Street proper is not any more responsible for such men than the Church, whose sacred precincts are used and abused by the same social pariahs in a similar manner. The Street is the victim of these adventurers, and has no more to do with nurturing and aiding them than the Church has." But he also argued that there was no substitute for integrity, morality, and fairness, even on Wall Street, and maybe especially on Wall Street. "No great business can be built up except upon honest and moral principles," he concluded. "It may flourish for a time, but it will topple down eventually. The very magnitude to which the business of Wall Street has grown is a living proof of its moral stamina. It is impossible, in the social and moral nature of things, to unite a large number of men, representing important material interests, except on principles of equity and fair dealing. A conspiracy to cheat must always be confined to a small number."

Clews had it exactly right. To wit, that while there can be no tolerance for bad behavior on Wall Street, the essential role that Wall Street plays in improving the lives of most Americans should not be thwarted as the result of the malfeasance of a few. That's as true today as it was more than 150 years ago.

Nowadays, what we think of collectively as "Wall Street" no longer exists on Wall Street. The only major Wall Street firm physically on Wall Street is not even American; it's German. In 2001, the U.S. securities arm of Deutsche Bank, the giant German bank, bought the elegant building, at 60 Wall Street, that was the headquarters of J.P. Morgan & Co., in the years before its merger with Chase Manhattan Bank. Meanwhile, the original headquarters of J.P. Morgan & Co., at 23 Wall Street, has been a vacant shell more or less since the bank sold it, in 2003, after the Chase merger to a real-estate developer, who then sold it five years later to an elusive Chinese billionaire, Sam Pa, for $150 million. Pa has done nothing with the building.

Wall Street today is more akin to a Disney theme park, or what a Disney park might be if it mythologized money-making. There is a Tiffany, a Hermès store, a BMW show-room, a Tumi luggage store, and an outlet for True Religion brand jeans. Fifty-Five Wall Street, which at one time was the headquarters of what is now Citigroup, is a branch of the Cipriani restaurant empire and is used for benefit dinners. Donald Trump claims to own 40 Wall Street, but, of course, that's not entirely true: He leases the building from the Italian businessmen who actually own the land underneath it. There are apartments for rent or sale at 37 Wall Street, at 63 Wall Street, at 75 Wall Street, at 95 Wall Street, and at 101 Wall Street.

But Wall Street remains a powerful symbol of American capitalism. Since September 11, cars are no longer permitted on Wall Street, and there are huge steel plates embedded into the road that are operated by motors that make sure that no unwanted vehicle ever again gets anywhere near the street or any of its historic buildings. The New York Stock Exchange, at the corner of Wall and Broad Streets, once the very embodiment of Wall Street, is mostly just a television backdrop for the business cable networks, such as Bloomberg, CNBC, and Fox Business, that use it as a set for their continuous coverage of the financial markets. Most trading is now done electronically.

To be sure, a number of important financial institutions—among them Goldman Sachs, American Express, and AIG—still have their headquarters in the vicinity of Wall Street. But by and large, Wall Street, the actual street itself, has become a mirage, a Potemkin village of a bygone era before computers and phones made physical interaction between traders and bankers somewhat obsolete. In mid-June 2016, Jim Cramer, the CNBC television anchor, tweeted a picture of the corner of Wall and Broad Streets, with the New York Stock Exchange in the background and the steps leading to the empty 23 Wall Street to the side. Right in the middle of the wonderfully manicured cobblestoned street—it used to be paved not so long ago—were four young women on yoga mats, striking a pose. "I remember when people used to work here," he wrote.

So remember this: Wall Street did not emerge fully

formed—and fully detestable—as some unknown villain's grand plan to empower the rich at the expense of the poor. Wall Street evolved over some four hundred years from the simple idea that people have different skills and different talents allowing them to produce different goods and services and that, one way or another, those goods and services need to be sold by the people who made them and bought by the people who want them. Period.

In many ways, Wall Street is the ultimate evolution of a weekend farmers' market, where fresh produce is brought to a central location in the middle of the town or city to be bought and sold. Everyone has to eat, but not everyone can be—or wants to be—a farmer. Inevitably, there will be a need to trade. On Wall Street, the fresh produce brought to market every day is money, or capital. Wall Street is in the business of matching the people with capital—such as savers and investors—with the people who want and need capital to grow their businesses to buy goods and services and to hire more employees. It's actually a relatively simple calculus—not complex at all, despite the plethora of Wall Street jargon—that has enabled millions of companies around the world, Apple, Google, and Amazon among them, to grow and to thrive and has helped to lift billions of people out of poverty and into the middle class and beyond. At its core, it's a remarkable bit of alchemy, one that should be celebrated, not despised, broken up, or dissolved. Doing so because you are angry at the behavior of a small misbehaving subset of bankers would be akin to the proverbial "throwing the baby out with the bathwater"—a massive overreaction to an entirely fixable problem.

CHAPTER 2

What Are Banks?

M ost people think banks and bankers get rich by not doing very much except moving money around and taking their cut. So let's get clear on what, exactly, banks actually *do*.

Commercial banks—places with physical branches where customers can deposit and cash checks and keep savings—engage in what is known as "fractional reserve banking," which sounds perplexing, I know. But the essential idea of it is simple: You keep your money at the bank by having a check directly deposited into an account or by going into a bank branch and depositing a check or cash into an ATM or with a bank teller. These days, of course, you can also use your iPhone to deposit checks. In return, the bank makes you two basic promises: One, and most important, is that your money will be there for you whenever you want to get it out; and, two, is that the bank will pay you what amounts to a small fee—these days a *very* small fee—for the use of your money, in the form of so-called interest payments. Checking accounts tend to offer depositors a lower rate of interest than do savings accounts on the theory that the access to the money in your checking account is more immediate than the access to the money in your savings account. But these are distinctions without much of a difference, and in any event the interest the bank pays on these accounts is virtually negligible. (In a surreal twist, in some countries at the moment, *you* pay the bank to keep your money "safe" for you.)

No matter how commercial banks dress up their behavior in a complicated lexicon, what depository institutions are in the business of doing every day is taking our deposits—for which they pay close to nothing at the moment—and then lending that money out to various corporations, governments, schools, foundations, and other organizations the world over that need or want that money—everything from General Electric to the National Basketball Association—in exchange for what they hope will be a profit based on the credit risk that business or organization poses. Commercial banks, of course, also make loans available to individuals to enable the purchase of homes, cars, and whatever else we use our credit cards to buy. The riskier the borrower's credit profile appears to be to the bank's credit-underwriting team, the higher the rate of interest the bank will charge a customer to borrow money. Theoretically, because banks can charge a higher interest rate to these borrowers, their profit potential to the banks should also be higher; that would be the case—and often is—except in the event of a "default" on the loan, when the threat of failure to pay back the loan looms. Then the losses on the loan can overwhelm the profit potential of these customers and result in losses that take with them years of anticipated profit. Deciding whether or not to lend money, based on the credit risk posed by the borrower, is a delicate, decidedly nontrivial balancing act.

In many ways, banking is the ultimate confidence game: The word "credit" derives from the Latin *credere*, which means "to believe" or "to trust." If a banker makes a loan, he or she believes that the borrower will pay the loan back with a sufficient level of interest (and fees) to allow the bank to make a profit. Talk about an act of faith! With ups and downs, this system of fractional reserve banking, incredibly, works fine until it doesn't. If we all start to fear that somehow we won't be able to get our money out of the bank when we want it, panic can set in very quickly. That panic becomes a self-fulfilling prophecy, causing the bank to fail because the ensuing stampede drains the bank's cash, or its ability to borrow, and it can no longer guarantee that we can get our money when we want it. When this happens—and thankfully it has been relatively rare in the scheme of things—it can be devastating to individual depositors, to the banks, and to the economy as a whole, both domestically and globally.

In other words, when a bank fails, it's a really big deal. For that reason, among others, in June 1933, in the wake of the Great Depression, the Federal Deposit Insurance Corporation, or FDIC, was created to protect the savings of individual depositors—the insurance now covers losses up to $250,000 per person at a single bank—as a way of trying to prevent a panic. It doesn't always work, of course, and banks still have a way of failing, but at least nowadays depositors have the confidence of knowing that all will not be lost.

These days, in part because of the 1999 repeal of the Glass-Steagall Act, the Depression-era law that separated commercial banking from investment banking, big banks do lots of other things, too. They manage people's money in order to try to increase their wealth. They manage money for other institutions, such as endowment and pension funds. They advise corporate CEOs on the buying and selling of companies—their own or others'—or various pieces of their businesses or others' businesses.

They underwrite stocks and bonds and trade them (in their securities subsidiaries) and make markets in individual stocks and bonds to give the market "liquidity," or the ability for customers to sell securities when we want to or have to. They make mortgage loans and car loans and issue credit cards. In fact, just as banks have been doing since the time of Hamilton and Burr, they have worked their way into every nook and cranny of our daily financial lives. By and large, this has been a good thing, making huge amounts of capital available at an affordable cost to people the world over who need it to start or to grow their businesses, to hire more employees, to pay them more money, to try to discover new products or new technologies, or to build new plants and buy new equipment. And it all starts with the simple idea that there are people who have money and there are people who want or need money.

A commercial bank is fundamentally nothing more than a middleman to put these two groups of people together in an efficient way: Investors get the financial return they feel is fair on their money, while the borrower gets access to capital at a cost he or she believes is fair, too. For its role in this interstitial world, the bank gets compensated in the form of fees and interest payments. Pretty straightforward. And unless there is some gross malfeasance, such as the Wells Fargo cross-selling scam that surfaced in 2016 wherein fifty-three hundred employees of the bank were fired for opening accounts that clients hadn't requested in order to get fees they hadn't earned, commercial banks do not generally draw the ire of the public. And that is because the public interacts directly with commercial banks and so understands what role they play: *They're the places where we go to get our money when we need it.*

Investment banks, such as Goldman Sachs and Morgan Stanley, are different. If you boil them down, though, they have always had the same goals as commercial banks: to make as much money for their employees and shareholders as possible. But until recently, the main difference was that investment banks were not permitted to take deposits. (After some 147 years, Goldman Sachs has finally decided there might be money to be made in accumulating retail deposits; it has no bank branches yet but rather is using the Internet to attract deposits. It also will use the Internet to make small loans to consumers for the first time.)

Investment banks were historically small and private, and the only capital they had available to them was the money their partners invested (a *hugely* important distinction from what they later became after they all started going public in 1970—a seminal development that we will get to soon enough). They could borrow money from other investors or from banks or from "the market," but unlike commercial banks they did not have a ready, and nearly inexhaustible, source of raw material—our deposits—to use to run their business. Investment banks had only the capital they could borrow or that their partners had invested. For the longest time, at investment banks, capital was an extremely dear, and often exceedingly rare, asset that was to be used prudently and judiciously to make money. Once that capital was depleted, it was usually too late for an investment bank to get more. There was basically no one around to save it from itself in times of trouble, and then it was gone. That's why Wall Street investment banks and brokerage firms have always been an especially dangerous enterprise; there was virtually no safety net for them. (This would begin to change, of course, in the late twentieth century and to reach its apotheosis for the first time ever with JPMorgan Chase's federally mandated bailout of Bear Stearns, in March 2008.)

Because there was no concern about losing the money ordinary people had deposited, investment banks had less of a public trust, or public responsibility to the commonweal. Commercial banks, over time, had become highly regulated and were expected to take far fewer risks than investment banks. At investment banks, because there were no depositors, only the capital that their partners invested or borrowed, a finely tuned culture of risk taking developed.

Now, this is the important part: For the longest time, in the investment banks, the risk taking was designed by its partners to be *prudent*. After all, while it is self-evident that the higher the risk, the higher the reward, partners at Wall Street investment banks did not want to take imprudent risks, because it was, largely, their own money. Making money, and a lot of it, was a good thing but not at the risk of putting their firms out of business and causing the partners to lose the capital—and the vast personal wealth—they had accumulated. Where we collectively lost our way with Wall Street was when the personal risk involved in financial bets became decoupled from the rewards for them by allowing bankers and traders to have access to and to use other people's money.

At the commercial banks, the *appearance* of stolidity and safety was crucial. That's why commercial banks were housed in big buildings made of stone, with gargantuan barrel-vaulted lobbies. It was important that from the very first moment a depositor walked through the revolving doors of a commercial bank, he or she felt an overwhelming sense of probity and caution.

At the investment banks, the message was different. They wanted to convey a measure of elitism and mysteriousness. Often the names of the firms did not appear on the buildings themselves. For most of its existence, the name of Goldman Sachs & Co., which was founded in 1869, never appeared anywhere on the facade of its headquarters. (It still doesn't.) Lazard Frères & Co., which was founded in New Orleans in 1848, never announced itself, either. If you didn't know it was there, you would be hard-pressed to find it. The message was clear: These businesses were not open to the general public. You were not welcome here.

Instead, investment banks catered to wealthy individuals, or to wealthy institutions or wealthy corporations that were looking for capital, advice, risk taking, or all of the above. What kept the investment banks on the straight and narrow path—at least theoretically anyway—was the daily, not inconsiderable chance that their partners' capital could be lost in one fell, stupid swoop, wiping away, in an instant, years of their own accumulated wealth. As the British wit Samuel Johnson supposedly noted in 1777, "Depend upon it, sir, when a man knows he is to be hanged in a fortnight, it concentrates his mind wonderfully." For the most part, the threat of daily annihilation kept the partners, and especially the traders they'd hired (imagine wiping out the personal wealth of your own boss because of a foolhardy bet), focused on taking prudent risks. Investment banks were riskier than commercial banks, surely, but the risks they were taking were not outrageous. As we shall see, that didn't come until the latter part of the twentieth century, when investment banks started going public, in effect using other people's money to take risks, rather than their partners', and upsetting the risk-reward balance that had existed on Wall Street for generations.

We need to return Wall Street to its days of prudent risk taking, where the leaders of the firms are held *personally* accountable for their bad behavior or foolish risk taking. That accountability, which used to be a given in the days when Wall Street was a series of undercapitalized private partnerships, has been totally lost in the modern era, when Wall Street has been transformed into behemoth public companies chock-full of other people's money and when a bonus culture has replaced the partnership culture. It's been said the three most dangerous words in the English language are "other people's money." We need to restore that accountability, and fast. If a banker or trader creates and sells a squirrelly financial product or makes a terrible and risky bet knowing full well when he or she did it that it was likely to go wrong, then there is little question, if convicted, that the expensive art should be sold off the walls in his or her home and that the home itself should be sold and the proceeds given to the victims.

There should be no equivocating on this point.

But then, we also must reward Wall Street for financial innovation because it is financial innovation that has led to what I call the "democratization of capital," the ability of more and more people to get access to capital at a fair price—whether in the form of a mortgage, an auto loan, or a credit card. These are important innovations that Wall Street has pioneered. They have given us the country and way of life that if it were suddenly stripped away, we would demand back. I mean, would you willingly go back to the Stone Age if you had the choice not to?

CHAPTER 3

Crises

There are two primary reasons most people cite for their ire directed at Wall Street: one, that the bankers, traders, and executives who work there recklessly cause financial crises that hurt the rest of us and, two, that they have figured out a way to get rich even when they lose lots of our money. Let's take a look at the first one and try to understand the nature of financial crises a little better.

Most important, as we have seen, scandals, panics, bubbles, and financial crises have been around for a long time. They are not Wall Street inventions. They are inventions of human nature. They have been around since before there was a Wall Street. So when we imagine that Wall Street is the sole cause of all financial calamities, that is not even remotely correct. It's a crucial point to remember. Of course, that doesn't mean Wall Street hasn't been involved in, or exacerbated, its share of financial turmoil. In March 1817, the brokers who had been trading for years on Wall Street at the Tontine Coffee House and under the buttonwood tree decided to organize themselves more formally in what they called the New York Stock and Exchange Board. They rented a room at 40 Wall Street and started meeting regularly. The purpose of the organization, the precursor of what became the New York Stock Exchange, or the NYSE, was for the president of the board to announce on a daily basis the prices for which the stocks of the companies listed on the exchange were bought and sold. It was also agreed that a penalty would be paid, upon conviction, for trading a "fictitious contract" at the board: expulsion.

In the early days of the exchange, only about thirty stocks and bonds were traded, including federal, state, and city bonds and the stocks of local banks and insurance companies. The formation of the stock exchange—bringing the trading of stocks and bonds indoors from out on the street—saw the concurrent creation and rise of the first so-called investment banks. The idea behind these banks, of course—no different from today—was to make money for the people who worked at them by raising capital for new businesses and to help those people who wanted to buy and sell the securities to do so. The capital raised helped to build the new nation's fledgling infrastructure—roads, bridges, canals, railroads—enabling the East to be connected to the West and the North to be connected to the South, creating jobs and wealth along the way.

But in 1819, America experienced the first—of what would be many—nationwide financial crisis, known as the panic of 1819, which then led to a short but painful two-year economic depression. The reasons for the panic were complex, of course—they always are—but the gist of the problem will seem familiar to those of us who lived through 2008. In the years after the War of 1812, the federal government and the banks it controlled were encouraging easy access to credit. One historian, Murray Rothbard, has called the era after the war and before the crash a "boom," with the Bank of the United States, aided and abetted by the U.S. Treasury, "acting as an expansionary, rather than as a limiting, force." The federal government was encouraging people to borrow and to invest. Land buyers were required to pay only a quarter of the purchase price within forty days, and Congress repeatedly postponed the penalty—forfeiture—for failure to pay what was owed within five years. Speculation and financial bubbles are nothing new.

A combination of factors—of course—conspired to burst the bubble. First, as investors sought to redeem their banknotes for cash, as was their right, banks became increasingly reluctant, or unable, to do so. Bank credit risk increased, and the banknotes began trading at a discount, itself a self-fulfilling prophecy that led to more and more people becoming worried about the soundness of the various banks that had sprouted up around the nation. Credit contracted, and the panic was on.

There would be many other "panics" in the nineteenth century—in 1857, 1873, 1884, and 1893, to name a few—and I won't go through them all here. According to the historian John Kenneth Galbraith, these "panics" occurred "roughly with the time it took people to forget the last disaster" and to start reengaging in the same typically human behavior once again. But in the midst of the turmoil of 1819 and beyond, Wall Street always found a way to recover, resuming its essential role at the center of finance in the young nation. The point is that throughout the many crises that have happened before and after the creation of Wall Street—and that will continue after you and I are long gone—it's important to keep in mind that these so-called big, evil banks raised, and continue to raise, the capital that built the nation, putting millions of people to work and lifting them out of poverty. Not even a century into its existence, America had become a magnet for oppressed people looking for a better life. Among the many reasons immigrants came here were the opportunities that existed to start and to build new businesses and to create wealth. Wall Street was at the center of those opportunities.

But there is no denying that Wall Street is particularly adept at fomenting or fueling a crisis, given how Darwinian a place it is. For every buyer of a stock or a bond, there is a seller. Every transaction has a customer, a client, a counterparty. For every winner, there is a loser. There is no way around it. So when the stampede toward bad or irrational behavior begins, there is often very little that can be done to stop it, although we like to think we can. That is just human nature.

The question in the United States has been how the consequences of the panics should be handled. Should the federal government intervene to save a bank or a Wall Street securities firm? Should the government have a role in encouraging the bad behavior of bankers through an implicit or explicit promise to bail them out if things go wrong—the so-called problem of creating a "moral hazard"? Go back 150 years, and the question was, should the federal government step in to save a failing railroad or a failing rope company? Usually, in our nation's history the answer has been to let a bank fail if it's going to fail or to let a railroad or a manufacturing company go into bankruptcy, and to let the market sort out the winners from the losers, to let the equity holders take it on the chin, and to let the creditors pick over the carcass. It seemed through much of our history, but obviously not all, a survival-of-the-fittest approach was best for Wall Street and for the rest of us. But during the financial crises of the twentieth and early twenty-first centuries, that approach was turned on its head and sorely tested.

Furthermore, as has been the case through most of our history, if there is clear wrongdoing by bankers and traders on Wall Street that results in scandals or financial crises, then prosecutions are not only warranted but also essential to send the stern message that such behavior cannot be tolerated. Too much is at stake for the financial markets to be manipulated without consequence. But it also makes no sense—as has been happening—to punish the economic prospects of the nation as a whole by overreacting to a panic and creating new regulations that prevent banks from performing their fundamental and crucial role in greasing the economy.

The panic of 1893, for instance, touched off a serious economic catastrophe and actually provided an interesting template for how the federal government might approach trying to resolve these crises. Some 660,000 people lost their jobs. It was an awful time. The banker J. P. Morgan, meanwhile, was busy with the reorganization of any number of failed railroads, thinking that putting them on a safer financial footing would restore jobs and give the economy a much-needed boost. He was also "keeping a watchful eye" on the gold supply of the U.S. Treasury as a continuous stream of Americans succeeded in depleting the gold reserves in exchange for their paper money.

Such was Morgan's power and prestige that he was able not only to move markets but also to bend the federal government to his will. The rescue that he devised in 1895 for the federal gold supply was a template that he would use again during and after the panic of 1907 and would lead to the creation, in 1913, of the Federal Reserve System, which remains—as the world saw in 2008 and beyond—the nation's lender of last resort. Morgan worked behind the scenes with government leaders in Congress and the Treasury to craft a gold-backed bond offering that would restore confidence in the nation's financial situation. The crisis had been averted, thanks to Wall Street. And an important new template had been established for a private market solution to a governmental financial crisis. J. P. Morgan's ability to raise capital when it was most needed had made solving the crisis possible. It would not be the last time.

Morgan came in for his share of accolades for devising a plan that avoided a further meltdown of the nation's financial markets, but he also came in for more than his

share of public condemnation. The late nineteenth century was also a populist moment in American history, and
the thought that the government had somehow colluded
with the most powerful Wall Street bankers to solve a
problem—from which, of course, they profited, although
by much less than was popularly believed—was too much
for people to stomach. Of course, the alternative—doing
nothing and letting America default on its debts—would
likely have been far worse than the private bond offering
that Morgan devised. But that's not the kind of argument
that wins much popular support, just as it's very difficult
for the American people to see the value in the bank
"bailouts" of 2008, which likely saved the financial system from a calamity far worse than that posed by the
Troubled Asset Relief Program, or TARP, which, as most
people remember, was the name of the $750 billion fed-
eral program designed to inject badly needed capital into
Wall Street's biggest banks at the most acute moment of
the crisis.

What people forget or don't know about TARP is that
the banks that received the billions of dollars in cash infusions from the government not only paid the loans
back with interest but also paid billions more to the government to extinguish the warrants, or small equity
stakes, that the government had taken in the banks as

compensation for the loans. In other words, the federal government profited massively from the TARP loans to the troubled banks.

At the same time, we must reckon—and I will soon enough—with the fact that a large slice of the blame for the 2008 financial crisis goes to the bankers who greedily created securities of questionable value and sold them off as proper investments around the world, only to watch them, predictably, default.

CHAPTER 4

The Story of the Central Bank

One of the reasons people hate Wall Street is its opac-
ity. It breeds distrust for obvious reasons. What the
hell goes on there? And so it's not a huge surprise that
people also are skeptical of the motives of the Federal Reserve, our centralized, national bank created more than a
century ago by powerful bankers meeting in an exclusive
club on a remote island. But it's essential to understand
its important role in monitoring, regulating—and, yes,
saving—our financial system as the need arises.

Because of the continuous turmoil of boom and bust
cycles during the nineteenth century and into the early
twentieth century, there was a belief that a more tightly
structured, centralized financial system should be put in
place. After all, the financial savior J. P. Morgan would

43

not live forever. Nor, as the nation's financial system grew alongside its economy, could one man be expected to rescue it time and time again. So, in November 1910, the Rhode Island senator Nelson Aldrich invited a select group of politicians and bankers to the exclusive Jekyll Island Club, off the coast of Georgia—J. P. Morgan had to arrange for permission to use the club—to discuss the idea of creating a central bank. The secret meeting included both Henry Davison, who by then was a senior partner at J.P. Morgan & Co., and Benjamin Strong, who was then at Bankers Trust, an affiliate of J.P. Morgan & Co. (and soon to be the first president of the Federal Reserve Bank of New York). Paul Warburg, another well-known banker of the era, was there, too. In order to avoid public consternation over the fact that powerful bankers and economists were working intimately with Senator Aldrich to create the nation's most powerful bank, the group convened using the ruse of duck hunting. On Aldrich's private railroad car, heading south, they addressed one another using first names only. Such was the concern about a leak that Davison and another banker, Frank Vanderlip, referred to each other as Orville and Wilbur, as in the Wright brothers.

During the next two weeks, instead of duck hunting, the bankers and the senator devised a system of twelve regional Federal Reserve banks, with a central governing board composed of not politicians but bankers, or men and women appointed by bankers. Their plan was meant to institutionalize what J. P. Morgan, the man, had done in the wake of both the 1893 and the 1907 crises. The new central bank would not only become the nation's lender of last resort but also strive to keep the financial system from overheating in the first place, or as a future Federal Reserve chairman, William McChesney Martin—the longest-serving Fed chair—once quipped, his job was to "take away the punch bowl just when the party gets going." Of the secret Jekyll Island meetings, Jean Strouse, one of J. P. Morgan's biographers, wrote that the men who were there "saw themselves not as serving their own interests, but as devising a financial system that would benefit the country as a whole."

But the politics of the time augured against the bankers' Jekyll Island solution. As ever, Congress feared putting Wall Street in control of something as crucial as the central bank. Much of that concern derived from the extraordinary concentration of financial might that had already ended up in the hands of a small group of powerful Wall Street bankers over the years, including (and especially) J. P. Morgan and his friends George Baker, at the First National Bank of New York, and James Stillman, at National City Bank of New York.

In the end, Wall Street's control of the Federal Reserve

System was limited but still highly influential. The Federal Reserve Act of 1913 created, as envisioned on Jekyll Island, a system of twelve regional Federal Reserve banks, which would be owned by the commercial banks in the various districts and have the ability to regulate the money supply, to tame inflation, and to serve as the nation's lenders of last resort during a financial crisis. The act also provided for a governing board—the Federal Reserve Board—based in Washington, the members of which were to be appointed by the president of the United States. Today, the chairman of the Federal Reserve Board is one of the most powerful individuals in Washington.

While it was true that the Federal Reserve System was created, in part, to combat the causes of the panic of 1907, Henry Goldman (the son of the founder of Goldman Sachs) seemed to have had an intuitive sense of the risks posed by actually turning to a reserve bank in an hour of need, in that it could cause, or exacerbate, a panic at the commercial bank seeking help. "The word 'aid' should be banished from our minds," he told two cabinet secretaries dispatched to seek his views at the time—the Treasury secretary, William McAdoo, and the agriculture secretary, David Houston. " 'Get aid.' That means alarm . . . It ought to be perfectly normal for a bank to go to a Reserve Bank and take discount, not in the sense of it being 'aid.' " Of course, it would not be normal for a bank to get "aid" from a reserve bank, but Henry Goldman understood the importance of having it *perceived* as normal, lest the financial concerns that drove the bank to get help in the first place become a self-fulfilling prophecy. (That very fear is what caused Hank Paulson, the Treasury secretary, to insist that all the big banks take TARP money during the 2008 financial crisis, whether they said they needed the money or not.)

It is easy to imagine that instead of McAdoo, Houston, and Goldman speaking in January 1914, it was Hank Paulson, Tim Geithner, and Lloyd Blankfein speaking in September 2008. Goldman agreed with the secretaries that the power to provide liquidity was essential, but he also warned presciently about the message that would be sent to the market when a bank actually tapped into a federal reserve bank. "I do believe that in business there are psychic factors which are so old and so ingrained in the human mind that no system can set them aside, and one is [the] capital strength of an institution," he said. The two cabinet secretaries agreed with Goldman.

"Sometimes it is nearly also psychic, is it not?" Houston wondered.

"I think there are times, and at the very critical times when it is all psychic," Goldman responded. "But up to that time, if the psychic operation is in the right direction, some of the cruelties which occurred here in 1907 would never have occurred." He told the cabinet secretaries they had in their "hands" the power to make the Federal Reserve banking system "a great vehicle for good." More than a hundred years later, whether the Federal Reserve System is a source of good or evil is much debated. But perhaps that's not the question we should be asking: It's important to keep in mind that the Federal Reserve is designed to act in the interest of banks, bankers, and the overall financial system by focusing on keeping inflation low and employment robust. If that happens to coincide with the interests of the American people, all the better.

For better or for worse, the creation of the Federal Reserve added to the growing fear among Americans that the banking system was designed to benefit the rich at the expense of the poor. After all, if in 1910 you had heard that a bunch of bankers and politicians were heading to a private club to devise a central bank, you might be entirely justified in feeling some amount of concern, rage even, about what exactly they were doing. It would be a rage not dissimilar to the one we felt after discovering that Dick Fuld, the CEO of Lehman Brothers, had hoovered more than $500 million out of the investment bank for himself in the years before driving Lehman into bankruptcy and our economy into turmoil. So the rage that many feel toward Wall Street and banks in general today is nothing new. But it is sometimes misguided and misdirected.

For as long as symbols of wealth, or wealth creation, have existed, they have been attacked. This desire to destroy something you believe to be evil, especially when it seems unattainable or only for others, is also a product of human nature.

In 1891, Henry Norcross, a "maniac," according to *The New York Times*, tried to murder the Wall Street financier Russell Sage in his second-floor office, at 71 Broadway, around the corner from Wall Street itself. Norcross entered Sage's office claiming to want to discuss railroad bonds with him and then demanded $1.2 million. Sage basically ignored the man. "Here goes!" Norcross said and then threw a satchel containing dynamite across the floor. Sage's secretary was killed, and eight others were injured. Norcross was killed. Sage was injured.

The next year, Alexander Berkman, a Russian anarchist, tried to kill Henry Clay Frick, the wealthy industrialist, but he was foiled. Berkman spent fourteen years in prison. But once released, he set off another bomb, killing four people but not its intended victim, John D. Rockefeller. (Berkman later committed suicide.) On July 3, 1915, fresh from exploding three sticks of dynamite

at the U.S. Capitol, Eric Muenter, a former Harvard professor and German sympathizer unhappy with America's
entry into World War I, made his way to J. P. Morgan Jr.'s
palatial mansion on an island off Glen Cove, New York,
on Long Island. Somehow Muenter gained access to
Morgan's house and fired several shots at the banker,
"two of which took effect," the *Times* reported. Muenter
was getting ready to fire additional shots at Morgan, when
the corpulent banker fell onto the gunman, pinning him
to the floor, where he was apprehended with help from
Morgan's family and the British ambassador to the
United States, with whom Morgan was lunching. "Kill
me," Muenter reportedly exclaimed upon being captured. "Kill me now! I don't want to live any more. I have
been in a perfect hell for the last six months on account of
the European war." He committed suicide in jail two days
later.

According to Michael Cannell, in his book *Incendiary*,
just before noon on September 16, 1920, a tired, old
horse-drawn covered wagon, "the kind used to deliver
milk and eggs," he wrote, slowly made its way to 23 Wall
Street, then the imposing domed headquarters of J.P.
Morgan & Co. at the corner of Wall and Broad Streets. The
intersection was known in financial circles as simply
"The Corner," and at the time it was the most important
address in finance. Across Broad Street from 23 Wall

Street was the headquarters of the New York Stock Exchange. On the other side of Wall Street was Federal Hall with its imposing bronze statue of George Washington, commemorating the place where our first president was inaugurated and the U.S. Congress was first convened.

The covered wagon came to a stop at the U.S. Assay Office, across the street from the headquarters of the most powerful bank in the world, blocking traffic. It was no coincidence. "Rather than pull out of the way, the driver stepped down to the footboard and slipped away," Cannell explained.

For some minutes the carriage stood still, the mare bowing and raising her head against the halter and shooing flies with her tail. Across the street, the Morgan partners assembled for their daily conference in a second-floor meeting room. Noon bells clanged from the spire of Trinity Church a few blocks to the west. A crowd of messenger boys, clerks and brokers streamed onto the street for lunch hour, unaware of the ticking muffled by a burlap tarp thrown across the wagon. Then, without warning, Wall Street erupted. A hundred pounds of dynamite shredded the horse and wagon. Window sash weights, sawed in half, were packed with the explosives. They sprayed pedestrians like jagged slugs, killing thirty. (Eight more would die in the hospital.) A concussive wave of flame rolled down Wall Street, knocking hundreds of pedestrians off their feet. The smoke cleared to reveal windows shattered as high as the twelfth floor. Horseflesh and human limbs lay in blood pools. A woman's severed head, hat and all, hung plastered to a wall. A Morgan banker [William Joyce] in charge of gold shipments was struck by a metal slug and slumped dead at his desk. Shards of jostled glass rained down on the scene below. Panicked survivors stampeded down Wall Street, trampling the wounded. Women who stayed behind to help tore their underwear into bandages and tourniquets. Bodies lay under white sheets at George Washington's bronze feet. Brokers wept. For a few hours the wealthiest intersection in the world looked like the bombed-out European cities New Yorkers had read about during World War 1.

It turned out that J. P. Morgan Jr. was traveling in Europe and not at 23 Wall Street that day. Nevertheless, thirty police detectives were immediately dispatched to protect Morgan's home on Madison Avenue. Pedestrians were not permitted to even walk in front of it.

Others were less lucky. Most of the people on Wall Street were middle-class clerks in the process of delivering physical securities from the stock exchange to the neighboring banks. After the explosion, the *Times* reported, "lay hundreds of men and women, most of them prone on their faces. Some were dead. Some writhed in agony. Some already were scrambling to their feet. Some were badly hurt and silent. Others screamed in pain and fright, some moaned, some cried for help for themselves. One little messenger, badly hurt, begged that someone would look after the little fortune of securities he clutched in an injured hand." It was 12:01 P.M., according to the stopped clock at the Assay Office building. "There seemed to be just that little instant after the dust cleared away when every one stood still, dazed, puzzled, frightened. Then as window after window, with now and then a chunk of stone, came tumbling down, they ran—ran in blind fear." Stock exchange trading was quickly halted for the day.

In the end, no one was held accountable for the explosion. And to this day, there is no memorial to the dead, no museum, and no way to recall what happened there, save for the still-unrepaired divots that pock the marble facade of the now-unoccupied 23 Wall Street, at nearly eye level.

In other words, rage against the machine is familiar ground. Populist ire directed at Wall Street bankers is nothing new. But populist ire directed at fat-cat bankers, whether it originates from anonymous anarchists or from the likes of Senators Sanders and Warren, accomplishes little, except to lead to a general misunderstanding of how Wall Street works. Wall Street is the engine of our economic growth. It is the way new businesses get started and get the capital to grow. It is often the way these businesses get the money they need to hire people and to pay them a decent wage. It often helps lead to a better way of life for billions of people the world over. The beautiful machine that provides this capital and fuels our economy should be fine-tuned rather than exploded. Ironically, it took the most devastating financial crisis in our nation's history—the Great Depression—to reveal how a gimlet-eyed president, Franklin Delano Roosevelt, could be a force for positive change on Wall Street, leading to nearly fifty years of prosperity uninterrupted by financial scandal. Would that we had a man—or woman— like FDR today leading the charge for the intelligent reform of our financial system.

CHAPTER 5

What We Can Learn from the Great Depression

The Great Depression was one of the few times in American financial history when there was not a countervailing force substantial enough to stop a panic. There was no J. P. Morgan in 1929, as there had been in 1895 and 1907. Nor did the Federal Reserve do the job it was designed to do, and it might, in fact, have exacerbated the crisis. Factories closed down. About one-quarter of the American workforce was unemployed, with scores of others barely scraping by with part-time work. Thousands of banks failed. No part of the country was spared, and the Great Depression's effects could be felt globally as well. Ultimately, it would take years for the economy to recover—until America joined World War II in earnest.

In November 2002, on the occasion of the ninetieth birthday of the Nobel Prize–winning economist Milton Friedman, Ben Bernanke, a Federal Reserve Board governor and its future chairman (before, during, and after the 2008 financial crisis), blamed the Fed's 1929 decision to make capital harder to get as one of the major causes for the depth and breadth of the Great Depression, or the Great Contraction, as Friedman and his co-author Anna Schwartz dubbed it. Bernanke, a former economics professor at Princeton, had devoted much of his academic life to the study of the Fed's role in causing the Great Depression before arriving at the Fed, and he was determined not to allow the same mistakes to be made on his watch.

In his speech honoring Friedman, Bernanke lavished praise on Friedman and Schwartz for their own ground-breaking research into the causes of the Great Depression that was included in their 1963 book, *A Monetary History of the United States*. "As everyone here knows, in their *Monetary History* Friedman and Schwartz made the case that the economic collapse of 1929–33 was the product of the nation's monetary mechanism gone wrong," Bernanke said. He noted that in the old days, before the creation of the Federal Reserve, "bank panics were typically handled by banks themselves," by cobbling together solutions, as Morgan had, that essentially prevented customers from withdrawing cash from an insolvent bank until another, more formidable bank could be found to take it over or that could provide cash to depositors. "Large, solvent banks had an incentive to participate in curing panics because they knew that an unchecked panic might ultimately threaten their own deposits," Bernanke said. One of the unintended consequences of the creation of the Federal Reserve System, Bernanke continued, was that the big banks no longer felt it was their responsibility, or in their interest, to save smaller banks, and so didn't, allowing the panic to spread. Bernanke also blamed 1929 Fed officials, who subscribed to the Darwinian view that weeding out weaker banks was good for the whole system.

At the end of his talk, Bernanke thanked Friedman and Schwartz and agreed with them that the responsibility for exacerbating the Great Depression—turning a cyclical economic bust into a crisis of unprecedented proportions—rightly belonged to the Federal Reserve. "Regarding the Great Depression," Bernanke concluded. "You're right, we did it. We're very sorry. But thanks to you, we won't do it again."

In 1933, for the first time in American history—in part because the Fed's policies had not solved the financial crisis (and in fact, as Bernanke argued, had exacerbated it)—the responsibility for trying to get the country out of its economic tailspin fell to the president of the United States, working in tandem with a sympathetic Congress. Fiscal policy would have to fill the void that monetary policy had created. (The exact opposite dynamic occurred in 2008, where Bernanke's creative monetary policies filled the massive void left by ineffectual, or nonexistent, fiscal policies after the implementation of the TARP.) As a result, Roosevelt redefined the role of government in American lives. The days of laissez-faire were over. Roosevelt used his first hundred days in office to try to restore the American people's confidence in their various institutions, including and especially the banks. As he said in a 1936 speech at Madison Square Garden, the hangover from the Roaring Twenties was severe. "Nine mocking years with the golden calf and three long years of the scourge!" he said. "Nine crazy years at the ticker and three long years in the breadlines! Nine mad years of mirage and three long years of despair!" As historians have well documented, from the outset Roosevelt was a whirlwind of tornadic activity.

What is less well known is how thoroughly Roosevelt savaged Wall Street, including in his first inaugural address, on Saturday, March 4, 1933. Everyone remembers FDR said that "this great Nation will endure as it has endured, will revive and will prosper" and that "the only thing we have to fear is fear itself—nameless, unreasoning, unjustified terror which paralyzes needed efforts to convert retreat into advance." But he then went on to excoriate bankers, who he suggested had caused the crisis through their own greed. "Practices of the unscrupulous money changers stand indicted in the court of public opinion, rejected by the hearts and minds of men," he said. "True they have tried, but their efforts have been cast in the pattern of an outworn tradition. Faced by failure of credit they have proposed only the lending of more money. Stripped of the lure of profit by which to induce our people to follow their false leadership, they have resorted to exhortations, pleading tearfully for restored confidence. They know only the rules of a generation of self-seekers. They have no vision, and when there is no vision the people perish. The money changers have fled from their high seats in the temple of our civilization. We may now restore that temple to the ancient truths. The measure of the restoration lies in the extent to which we apply social values more noble than mere monetary profit." He urged the American people to pursue a simpler, nobler set of values. "Happiness lies not in the mere possession of money," he continued, "it lies in the joy of achievement, in the thrill of creative effort. The joy and moral stimulation of work no longer must be forgotten in the mad chase of evanescent profits. These dark days will be worth all they cost us if they teach us that our true destiny is not to be ministered unto but to minister to ourselves and to our fellow men."

Roosevelt promised to reform Wall Street to prevent "a return of the evils of the old order" and added that "there must be a strict supervision of all banking and credits and investments" and "there must be an end to speculation with other people's money." The latter problem remains unsolved today.

Less than a week after his speech, Roosevelt submitted the Emergency Banking bill to Congress, which passed it the same day. The new law was designed to allow bank regulators to figure out which banks were solvent and could reopen, with the help of an injection of liquidity from the Fed, and which were not and would need to remain closed. Just as Bernanke would do after the 2008 financial crisis—in the form of the so-called Quantitative Easing program—the Fed injected capital into struggling banks by buying assets from them. The Fed paid full price for Treasury securities held by the banks and less than full price for other assets, such as the bonds of railroad companies and retailers, giving the solvent banks the much-needed cash to meet the demands of their depositors. National and state banks could reopen only after being licensed by the Treasury. Roosevelt additionally reauthorized the Reconstruction Finance Corporation—in some ways the precursor of TARP—and allowed it to invest in the debt and equity of banks in order to re-capitalize them and to put them on a more financially sound footing. *The New York Times* described Roosevelt's actions as the "most drastic" ever taken by the federal government in peacetime.

To explain himself, Roosevelt took to the radio air-waves. On March 12, in his first of many "fireside chats," for which he would become justly famous, the president explained how he intended to restore confidence to the banking system—confidence, he said, that had to come from the American people themselves. His understand-ing of the banking system and its inherent risks was lucid. He endeavored to make a complex subject—how banks work and why they are important—understandable to the millions of Americans no doubt baffled about why they had lost or could not get access to their savings or who had lost them by depositing their money in banks that failed. It was a tough sell. But he did it brilliantly.

FDR said

First of all, let me state the simple fact that when you deposit money in a bank the bank does not put the money into a safe deposit vault. It invests your money in many different forms of credit—in bonds, in com-mercial paper, in mortgages, and in many other kinds of loans. In other words, the bank puts your money to work to keep the wheels of industry and of agriculture turning round. A comparatively small part of the money that you put into the bank is kept in currency—an amount which in normal times is wholly sufficient to cover the cash needs of the average citizen. In other words, the total amount of all the currency in the country is only a comparatively small proportion of the total deposits in all the banks of the country.

But when everyone wants his or her money at the same time, all hell breaks loose. If banks tried to meet the extraordinary demand for cash by, say, selling some of their longer-term assets, the prices for these assets would fall, exacerbating the panic. In other words, Roosevelt said, it's the same old story, the Achilles' heel of the banking system, which is designed to fund long-term assets (loans) with short-term money (customer deposits). It all works just fine as long as everyone doesn't want his or her money at the same time. In 1932 and 1933, the problem was that everyone *did* want his or her money at once, and about half the banks in the country failed. In 2008, the same thing happened again—long-term assets were being financed in the short term—but with a significant twist: This time, the run on the banks was fomented by institutions, not individuals, desperate to get their money out of what they thought were insolvent institutions, which, of course, exacerbated their decline. A vicious cycle, once again. (Ironically, individuals were far less panicked in 2008 than they were in 1933 because in the meantime FDR had created the Federal Deposit Insurance Corporation, which, as was discussed earlier, now insures up to $250,000 of an individual's money in a single bank account at banks covered by the FDIC.)

In his March 12 fireside chat, Roosevelt explained that by March 3, the day before his inauguration, "scarcely a bank in the country was open to do business." The next day, Monday, March 13, he announced that, after being certified as healthy by the Treasury, banks in the 12 cities where there were also Federal Reserve banks would be allowed to reopen. On Tuesday, banks in another 250 cities would be allowed to reopen. Slowly but surely, he said, all healthy banks would be allowed to reopen, and, if appropriate, the unhealthy banks would be recapitalized using the expanded power of the Reconstruction Finance Corporation, which Herbert Hoover created in 1932. Roosevelt said most everyone would get his or her money back. There was no reason for continued panic. He warned hoarders not to hoard because "the phantom of fear will soon be laid" to rest and said that it was safer to keep money in a reopened bank than in a mattress at home.

He then reiterated the problem and how important it

was for the American people to have renewed faith in the banking system, thanks to extraordinary measures taken by the federal government to restore confidence. "We had a bad banking situation," Roosevelt said.

Some of our bankers had shown themselves either incompetent or dishonest in their handling of the people's funds. They had used the money entrusted to them in speculations and unwise loans. This was, of course, not true in the vast majority of our banks, but it was true in enough of them to shock the people of the United States for a time into a sense of insecurity and to put them into a frame of mind where they did not differentiate, but seemed to assume that the acts of a comparative few had tainted them all. And so it became the government's job to straighten out this situation and to do it as quickly as possible. And that job is being performed.

Renewed confidence was the key. "There is an element in the readjustment of our financial system more important than currency, more important than gold, and that is the confidence of the people themselves," the president concluded. "Confidence and courage are the essentials of success in carrying out our plan. You people must have faith; you must not be stampeded by rumors or guesses.

Let us unite in banishing fear. We have provided the machinery to restore our financial system; and it is up to you to support and make it work. It is your problem, my friends, your problem no less than it is mine. Together we cannot fail." Wouldn't it be refreshing if someone today, of nearly the stature of FDR's, conducted regular forthright conversations with the American people about how the economy is performing in an effort to pry open the black box of Wall Street, instead of the opaque gobbledygook that slithers out of the mouths of the Federal Reserve governors and of our leading economists?

FDR's unusual gambit worked. On March 13, many banks in the Federal Reserve cities reopened. Ten days later, something like 80 percent of the nation's banks were open for business. Of course, Roosevelt was just getting started. The United States officially abandoned the gold standard on April 19. On May 27, FDR signed the Securities Act of 1933, which required that investors receive important financial and other information from companies concerning securities offered for sale (hence the Apple IPO prospectus). Untruthful statements were a violation of the law. On June 16, FDR signed the Banking Act of 1933 (generally known as the Glass-Steagall Act), giving Wall Street banks one year to choose between commercial banking and investment banking. The law, barely thirty-seven pages long, was premised on the idea that in the years leading up to the Great Depression, commercial banks—which, as we learned earlier, are the institutions in the business of accumulating your deposits and then turning around and lending that money out—were taking way too many risks with their depositors' money and had their collective fingers in way too many pies. A year later, FDR signed the Securities Exchange Act of 1934, creating the Securities and Exchange Commission to regulate virtually every aspect of Wall Street and to require public companies to file quarterly financial statements that the SEC would then approve. The 1934 act also regulated the trading of securities on Wall Street in the secondary market.

It was a regulation bonanza the likes of which Wall Street had never seen before and has never really seen since. But such was the extent of financial catastrophe that there seemed to be little disagreement about the need for heavy-duty reforms.

Wall Street would never be the same. As hard as it might be to believe today, the provisions in the Banking Act of 1933 that forced the separation of commercial banking from investment banking were not particularly controversial. It seemed like a pretty obvious solution at the time. There was general agreement that commercial banks should not be using their customers' hard-earned deposits to invest in risky equity securities, to buy ownership stakes in companies in tangential industries, or to partake in the underwriting of debt and equity securities. For most banks, the choice between investment banking and commercial banking was not difficult. Firms such as Goldman Sachs, Lehman Brothers, Kidder, Peabody, and Lazard Frères stuck to their investment banking knitting. Other firms, such as J.P. Morgan & Co., split itself up, creating both J.P. Morgan & Co., a commercial banking enterprise, and Morgan Stanley & Co., an investment bank.

At the time, separating investment banking from commercial banking was more akin to separating a yolk from the white; today, it would be like unscrambling an egg.

But that seemingly insurmountable problem has not kept politicians who should know better from trying to do it anyway. They are profoundly wrong to think that what worked in the 1930s, when Wall Street was a collection of undercapitalized private firms, would work again today, when Wall Street is the supreme force dominating global finance.

Senator Elizabeth Warren is leading the charge in Washington to return Wall Street to a bygone era. She wants to break up the big banks—any bank with more than $50 billion in assets is in her sights—and in 2013 she joined with a bipartisan group of her fellow senators, including John McCain, Maria Cantwell, and Angus King, to introduce a bill she called the 21st Century Glass-Steagall Act—an homage to the original law passed eighty years earlier. It was created, she stated, to make the financial system safer. In fact, it would do nothing of the sort.

The goal, Senator Warren wrote in the bill, was "to reduce risks to the financial system by limiting banks' ability to engage in activities other than socially valuable core banking activities" and "to protect taxpayers and reduce moral hazard by removing explicit and implicit government guarantees for high-risk activities outside of the core business of banking." Senator Warren's bill went nowhere in the 113th Congress, in large part because it was simply a bad idea. So she and Senator McCain reintroduced it in June 2015. "Shattering the wall dividing commercial banks and investment banks, a culture of dangerous greed and excessive risk-taking has taken root in the banking world," Senator McCain said in a statement explaining why he thought the wall should be rebuilt. "Big Wall Street institutions should be free to engage in transactions with significant risk, but not with federally insured deposits." (During his presidential campaign, Donald Trump also spoke about reintroducing a version of Glass-Steagall, although it does not seem to be on his list of postinauguration legislative priorities.)

Despite the relentless rhetoric from clueless politicians, the fact that commercial banks are in the investment banking business and investment banks are in the commercial banking business had almost nothing to do with the causes of the financial crisis of 2008. The truth is that the most acute problems in the years leading up to the financial crisis occurred in what we would traditionally think of as pure investment banks—Bear Stearns, Lehman Brothers, Merrill Lynch, and Morgan Stanley—which, thanks to Wall Street's wayward incentive system, had gone hog wild in the manufacture and sale of mortgage-backed securities, billions of dollars of which they allowed to build up on their balance sheets. When the banks' short-term lenders no longer wanted to use these assets as collateral for overnight loans, the investment banks could not finance their daily operations and up came the white flags of surrender. As we all remember, JPMorgan Chase rescued Bear Stearns, and Bank of America rescued Merrill Lynch.

If Glass-Steagall were reimposed, JPMorgan Chase's rescue of Bear Stearns and Bank of America's rescue of Merrill Lynch would have been prohibited. Just contemplate the idea of Lehman Brothers, Bear Stearns, and Merrill Lynch in bankruptcy at the same time. You can bet that Morgan Stanley and Goldman Sachs would have also filed for bankruptcy in Senator Warren's world, too, because the Federal Reserve essentially rescued both of those investment banks, in late September 2008, by allowing them to become bank holding companies. That gave them access to short-term funding from the Fed, a huge benefit because other forms of short-term financing in the markets were drying up. (After the Fed allowed Goldman Sachs and Morgan Stanley to become bank holding companies, each quickly obtained a lifesaving equity investment: Goldman from Warren Buffett and the public market; Morgan Stanley from a large Japanese bank.)

The financial chaos that would have resulted from having most of Wall Street in liquidation not only might have been useful to Senator Warren politically—why else would she advocate it?—but also would have likely brought the financial system to a halt and have been a disaster for the American economy and the American people. Would that have decreased risk, as Senator Warren argued, or increased it dramatically, with everyone acting out of even deeper desperation? The answer is obvious. That small fact aside, there are other, equally important reasons why reinstating a version of the Glass-Steagall Act makes little sense beyond that it would try to solve a problem that doesn't exist. Breaking up the big banks into smaller pieces would also be extraordinarily difficult, time-consuming, and costly. Over the years, Wall

Street has become increasingly integrated along product lines. Sure, separating the covalent bonds that bind products and bankers together could be done but only at great cost over many years. Warren's bill would be a boon to high-priced lawyers, accountants, and consultants but to few others. But, again, to what end?

Breaking up the big banks would also destroy Wall Street's leadership position in world finance—no little thing (although that might be just what Senator Warren wants to do). Not only has Wall Street long been the envy of governments around the world for its ability to help companies raise capital, get advice about mergers and acquisitions, and manage wealth; it is also an employment- and wealth-creation machine that has led to billions of people and companies paying trillions of dollars in taxes every year. Year after year, Wall Street's banks are the world leaders in raising capital and in providing corporate advice, generating billions of dollars in revenue. Left in the dust, consistently, are European banks and Chinese banks. Why would it make any sense at all for the U.S. Congress to pass a law that would destroy one of America's leading industries and put its own companies at a competitive disadvantage, to say nothing of the tax revenue that would be lost in the wake of the Great Unwinding of Wall Street? It's a recipe for nothing short of revolution. If the Russians, say, deployed a computer virus that destroyed the infrastructure of Wall Street, we would consider it an act of war. Why are we considering a congressional act that would have the same effect?

Then there is the fact that Wall Street's clients want Wall Street to offer them as many products as possible, each with seamless, world-class execution. This is why they choose Wall Street's banks to help them in the first place, as opposed to German banks or Chinese banks. This so-called one-stop-shop approach means clients can get the financing and advice they need from one firm, or a small group of firms, where they have trusted, decades-long relationships and where they can be certain that they will get what they need in a confidential, reliable way. AT&T's announced $85 billion acquisition of Time Warner is a perfect example of why these two companies chose Wall Street firms both to finance the proposed deal and to advise them on it. They could get exactly what they wanted from the American banks they hired. They could have selected anyone they wanted in the world to help them on the deal, and they chose the American banks, and only American banks. There is a reason Wall Street banks dominate the so-called league tables of global finance year after year. Despite the mistakes—and there have been far too many of them in recent years, no question—Wall Street is the best at what it does. Why destroy America's dominant position in world finance—a position that clients seek out regularly and that took centuries to establish—to prove a political point? It doesn't make any sense. And just to reiterate—the causes of the 2008 financial crisis had nothing to do with the fact that there wasn't a wall separating commercial banking from investment banking, so why in the world would the right answer be to erect a new one now?

Even if reinstating Glass-Steagall is a boneheaded idea, Senator Warren is right about one thing: There's no question Wall Street needs intelligent reform. The question is how to go about doing it. I will get to the answer to that question after a brief diversion into how it came to pass that Wall Street was able to transmit its problems to the rest of us, with such devastating consequences.

CHAPTER 6

The Problem with Going Public

On the afternoon of May 22, 1969, Dan Lufkin, the thirty-six-year-old cofounder of a small research-focused investment banking and brokerage firm, Donaldson, Lufkin & Jenrette, or DLJ, walked into his first board of governors meeting at the august New York Stock Exchange, then, as now, located at the corner of Broad and Wall Streets, carrying with him a copy of a document that he had filed two hours earlier with the SEC. It was the first step in the process that would transform DLJ from a ten-year-old private partnership, with its stock owned by the firm's partners and their friends, into a public company with shares that could be bought or sold by anyone willing to do so. It also would allow DLJ to get greater access to more affordable and badly needed capital than its partners would otherwise be able to provide.

DLJ "is the first member corporation of the New York Stock Exchange to offer its equity securities to the public," the firm proclaimed on the cover of its prospectus. DLJ's decision to sell a portion of its equity to the public—it was hoping to raise $24 million—was a direct challenge to a nearly two-hundred-year-old NYSE rule that prohibited member firms from selling stock to the public because the NYSE had to approve all stockholders of a member firm. Obviously, with a public company's stock being bought and sold nearly every hour of every day, the NYSE would no longer be able to approve, or not, the DLJ stockholders.

Wall Street would never be the same. And not necessarily for the better.

That was just fine with the brash and aggressive founders of DLJ, who were eager to challenge the status quo on Wall Street and everything that it meant to be a Wall Street securities firm. Ever since the three founders met at Harvard Business School and decided to start a brokerage firm together with around $500,000 in cash, they always hoped to attract permanent capital by turning to the public as investors. DLJ was a small but very profitable firm, as the document Lufkin had with him attested—

revenue in 1969 was $30.4 million and pretax income was nearly $14 million, a 46 percent profit margin, facts that competitors devoured—and the three partners knew that to continue growing and to take advantage of the myriad business opportunities available to them, they needed more capital. (For instance, DLJ had just bought Louis Harris and Associates, the polling firm, for eighty thousand shares of stock.) They had always wanted to go public, and this was their chance, especially because Lufkin had grown tired of the years the NYSE spent study-ing the issue, without making any progress.

Lufkin knew that going public was against the NYSE rules and that DLJ could be kicked out of the NYSE club, which, of course, had the potential to damage materially its future profitability. The firm hoped that the board of governors would somehow see the situation its way and allow it to remain an NYSE member and also to go public, especially in light of another burgeoning crisis—the so-called back-office crisis, when many brokerage firms could not process their paperwork fast enough and then failed—that was exposing how woefully Wall Street was undercapitalized. "However," the firm said in the pro-spectus, "DLJ's ability to avail itself of opportunities for continued growth is a more important consideration. Capital additions can be effectively utilized immediately and are essential to the maintenance and improvement of its competitive position." To try to see if he could ease a path forward for DLJ's IPO, Lufkin had dinner the night before the board of governors' meeting with his close friend Bunny Lasker, the NYSE board chairman, at Lasker's Park Avenue apartment. Lufkin told Lasker about the plan for the DLJ IPO, which until then had been a carefully guarded secret.

"You're crazy," Lasker told him.

"I hope not," Lufkin replied. "Well, Bunny, we've been studying this thing for five years and nothing's getting done, so nothing is changing about that conclusion, but it's time we get something done."

Lasker replied, "Well, I can't support you. If it comes up at the meeting tomorrow, I'm just going to say, 'We're fortunate to have Dan Lufkin, who will be able to explain this.' That's all I'm doing."

The next day, a very nervous Lufkin distributed the IPO documents to the assembled governors. They asked the requisite questions about what could possibly have possessed Lufkin and his partners to make such a rash decision. He explained how DLJ needed a permanent source of capital to grow, to make acquisitions, to redeem the stock of partners looking to leave the business, and to be able to attract new partners. It all made sense, but it was absolute heresy.

The leaders of the NYSE, while appalled by DLJ's gambit, had little choice but to follow the NYSE's bylaws for amending its constitution. They knew, deep down, that in order to continue financing the growth of the country's great businesses, Wall Street needed more capital. The easiest and cheapest way for Wall Street to get the capital it needed was from the public, just as Wall Street's corporate clients had been doing for more than a century. Soon after DLJ filed its IPO prospectus with the SEC, Lufkin proposed amendments to the NYSE's constitution that would allow member firms to go public, as, of course, nearly any other corporation could do, with Wall Street's help. DLJ was simply trying to do for itself what Wall Street had been doing for other American businesses for nearly two centuries: helping them to raise the capital they needed to grow their businesses from the people who had capital they wanted to invest. And for many of the same reasons: DLJ needed the capital, which was more plentiful and cheaper than private capital, to grow its business, to hire more people, and to consider getting into new business lines.

On April 10, 1970, nearly a year after first filing its IPO prospectus with the SEC, DLJ pulled it off, raising $12 million from the public and as a result fundamentally altering how Wall Street has functioned ever since. "Going public changed Wall Street permanently and forever," Richard Jenrette (the *J* in DLJ) told the *Times*. "If

Wall Street had remained in a private mode, it would have acted like a club and been so vastly undercapitalized that someone would have taken it over long ago. There would have been no alternative but to have let the [commercial] banks take over"—something that the Glass-Steagall law, of course, had made illegal. The truth was going public made perfect sense for DLJ and for the many Wall Street firms—nearly every one—that followed its lead.

The problem is that we are still dealing with the unintended consequences of the DLJ IPO to this day. And, of course, because it was 1970, very few people, if any, were paying attention to what a small private partnership on Wall Street was trying to do to change the system. And honestly, the importance of the DLJ IPO has still not been fully appreciated. But it was a seminal event.

Whereas for more than 150 years Wall Street firms had relied on the prudent use of their partners' capital to take risks—which nonetheless occasionally went awry—and to run their businesses, knowing full well that a single mistake could spell the end for their firms, as well as threaten whatever fortunes they had personally built up over the years, the move by DLJ was destined to change the whole calculus of Wall Street. If DLJ were successful, if the public's capital could be substituted for partners' capital, if the public's legal liability for mistakes could be substituted for the partners' legal liability for mistakes, there would be no telling what the consequences would be both for Wall Street and for everybody who relied on Wall Street to raise capital, to provide liquidity in the buying and selling of stocks and bonds, and to help individuals manage and grow their wealth. Although it was unlikely the founders of DLJ could have anticipated all of what its IPO would unleash over the next nearly fifty years, they must have had some inkling that by substituting a bonus culture—where bankers, traders, and executives demand to be paid for the revenue they generated in their various product lines—for the long-standing partnership culture—where the individual partners of the firm collaborated to make sure only prudent risks were taken in order to ensure there would be annual pretax profits for them to divide—Wall Street would never be the same.

And the behavior of Wall Street bankers, traders, and executives since 1970 as one firm after another followed DLJ's lead, has proved unequivocally that neither Wall Street nor much of the world's economy would be left unchanged. People are pretty simple; they do what they are rewarded to do. Thanks to the DLJ IPO, bankers and traders were being rewarded to take outsized risks with *other* people's money and with very little financial accountability when things went wrong, as happens with far more frequency and severity than anyone cares to acknowledge. Before the DLJ IPO, mistakes made by partners at individual firms could be personally devastating for them, causing one existential crisis after another, if not causing the firm to go out of business.

After the DLJ IPO, the stakes were very different. Firms had much easier access to capital—in the forms of both debt and equity—and that capital largely came from outside investors, often leaving the original partners of the firm very wealthy and with little of their own capital left at risk in the firm. The idea of essentially playing with the house's money and being rewarded for it would lead Wall Street's numerous critics to refer to it as a casino, where the house always finds ways to win. It forever altered the reward system that had been so carefully calibrated over the centuries to encourage prudence over wanton risk taking and to emphasize long-term profitability over short-term greed.

Ultimately, the unintended consequences of the DLJ IPO would be devastating. In October 1970, Weeden & Co. followed DLJ's lead and went public. Then the floodgates opened. In December 1970, a small firm, Pressman, Frohlich & Frost, went public by merging with another, already public financial firm. Its chairman, Stanton Pressman, told *The New York Times* that the times they were a-changing, and fast. "Without major public capital," he said, "I think member firms are going to find themselves very hard-pressed to compete. The little grocery store in this business is just not going to make it. You've got to have the ability to do much more."

Pressman was right (although his firm is long defunct). In April 1971, Merrill Lynch, the largest brokerage firm on Wall Street, announced its plans for a $120 million IPO. *The New York Times* called it a "milestone" that would "set the standard" for other Wall Street firms to go public. The news was on the front page of the paper, its lead story of the day. In September 1971, Bache & Co., the nation's second-largest brokerage, announced plans for its own IPO, in part to be able to compete better with Merrill Lynch, which had increased its capital by nearly 50 percent with its successful IPO. Suddenly the remaining private partnerships found themselves at a significant competitive disadvantage, having to compete against their better-capitalized peers. What had been for nearly two hundred years an industry of small, poorly capitalized private partnerships was being rapidly transformed into a group of bigger, more powerful public firms with easy access to cheap capital. The existential question for the firms that remained private was whether they intended to try to compete with their public peers or to remain small and focused.

But, truthfully, there was very little choice, especially if firms wanted to compete in the underwriting or trading businesses, which required tremendous amounts of capital. In 1981, Salomon Brothers, the big bond house, merged with Phibro Corporation, a publicly traded commodities dealer, and eventually became Salomon Inc., a public company. Also in 1981, American Express bought Shearson Loeb Rhoades, a brokerage firm, and Prudential Insurance bought Bache & Co. In 1984, American Express added Lehman Brothers to its stable. In 1985, Bear Stearns & Co. went public. Morgan Stanley went public in 1986. In 1994, American Express spun off the combined Lehman and Shearson to the public. After years of internal debate, which had begun to take on the feel of a Shakespearean drama, Goldman Sachs, the most profitable and envied Wall Street firm, decided to go public in May 1999, making the partners lucky enough to be there on that day extremely rich. Even Lazard Frères & Co., which prided itself on its quirkiness and iconoclasm—and its intense privacy—went public in May 2006. The partnership culture that had dominated and molded Wall Street behavior for nearly two hundred years was over. Wall Street would never be the same, nor for that matter would the American economy it supposedly served.

It would take a decade or so, but by the late 1980s Wall Street had been utterly transformed from a series of relatively small, undercapitalized private partnerships, where the partners of the firm supplied the sparse capital needed and faced the risk of losing it every day, to a group of fast-growing publicly traded companies, where capital was relatively cheap and relatively abundant and where there was a distinct disconnect between the people who supplied the capital—the shareholders and creditors—and the people who managed and worked at the firms. The fundamental link between capital, risk taking, and accountability had been severed, never to return—or not yet anyway. As a result, the *culture* of Wall Street was forever transformed from small, intimate petri dishes of greed and caution, where prudent risk taking was celebrated in hopes of generating sufficient pretax profits on an annual basis that could then be distributed to the partners, into a Darwinian free-for-all, where bankers, traders, and executives were rewarded for taking big risks with other people's money in the hope of being able to justify to a division manager that they deserved—indeed *must* have—multimillion-dollar annual bonuses. In short order, Wall Street's incentive system—what people got rewarded to do every day—went from being focused on a sense of collective benefit, where the partners risked on a daily basis nearly everything they had worked for in their lives, to one where, despite corporate window dressing to the contrary, each individual's annual bonus discussion was based largely on how much revenue had been generated in the previous year. It was a relatively simple calculus: Those bankers, traders, and executives who had generated the most revenue were rewarded with the biggest bonuses, the amount of which always managed to seep out for everyone to know. Those who had not produced the revenue were given small bonuses or fired. The new culture on Wall Street was one that encouraged swinging for the fences—taking big risks with other people's money—in hope of getting a big annual bonus. The message was clear: Either produce or you're out. And we all know where that has led us.

If one had to point to when it all started going terribly wrong, there is no question that it was the moment the investment banks went public.

CHAPTER 7

Innovation

You also should understand the other ways going public lic changed Wall Street. Easy access to cheap capital created a spate of incredible financial products that seemed to be invented virtually out of thin air at around the same time and that resulted in huge, new sources of revenue for Wall Street. For more than a century, there had been virtually no innovation on Wall Street. Every firm did pretty much exactly the same things with its limited capital: underwrite debt and equity offerings for its corporate clients as well as for cities, states, and federal and foreign governments and advise on the buying and selling of companies. Some Wall Street firms also managed people's money, trying to help them increase their wealth.

Suddenly, though, in the late 1970s and early 1980s, boring old Wall Street was not so boring anymore. Wall Street exploded out of the "Dark Ages," as Lazard Frères senior partner Felix Rohatyn had described the years in and around the back-office crisis of the late 1960s. Wall Street's animal spirits were raging again. These innovations could in part be traced back to the changed compensation system. Given how much Wall Street was suddenly able to pay people, the best and the brightest the world over started flocking to Wall Street. Wall Street was once a haven for family members with nothing better to do or for people who ended up in finance serendipitously. But starting in the mid-1970s, it became *the* magnet for graduating MBAs from the best business schools in the country, who quickly realized that Wall Street was the place to go for millions of dollars in compensation without having to risk one's own capital in the process. Wall Street— whether at big banks or hedge funds or private-equity funds—still attracts risk-averse people who are confident that they can make a fortune for themselves using other people's money.

Also in the mid-1970s, Wall Street began diversifying its hires, looking beyond MBAs to recruit brilliant PhDs in mathematics and physics, as well as a group of literal rocket scientists, to design new products. The first important innovation came in the market for home mortgages. Once upon a time, a local banker would provide a mortgage to his neighbor so that he could buy his own home and have a small slice of the American Dream. Before making the loan, the banker would know all about the borrower—his reputation, his standing in the community, his income, his net worth, and, importantly, his prospects for repaying the borrowed money. That mortgage would then sit on the local bank's balance sheet for thirty years, unless paid off sooner, and the bank's profits—*its* ability to make money from money—would be determined in large part by how good a credit risk the borrower turned out to be. If he paid the interest and principal on the mortgage on time, it was a good bet the loan would be profitable for the bank. Knowing your customer was good business.

That tried-and-true formula began to change in 1977 when the Brooklyn-born Lew Ranieri came up with the clever idea that everyone—the borrower, the bank, and of course Salomon Brothers, his employer—would be better off if there were a way to buy up the mortgages from the local banks and package them all together, thereby spreading the risk presented by any one borrower across a broad portfolio of borrowers. Then the resulting securities backed by these mortgages could be sold in pieces to investors the world over, with varying rates of interest depending on an investor's risk appetite. Ranieri, who had started at Salomon in the mailroom, assembled a team of PhDs to package, slice, and sell the mortgages; to him, mortgages were "just math" and represented streams of cash flows that investors might want to buy. This powerful idea—later dubbed securitization—was a once-in-a-generation innovation that revolutionized finance. Ranieri's idea caught on and, so the theory goes, helped reduce the cost of mortgages for borrowers all over the country, because the market for the mortgages was far more liquid packaged up as securities than when they simply sat on a bank's balance sheet tying up capital for thirty years. Ranieri brought a similar magician's skill to the streams of payments consumers made to pay off their car loans and credit-card bills, payments that eventually were also securitized and sold off to investors worldwide. Salomon Brothers—and Ranieri—made a fortune implementing Ranieri's insight.

In typical Wall Street fashion, other firms deconstructed Ranieri's alchemy and began copying what he had done, competing with Salomon Brothers to underwrite mortgage-related securities. For a while, everyone on Wall Street who touched a home mortgage got fabulously rich. In 2004, *Businessweek* dubbed Ranieri "one of the greatest innovators of the past 75 years." But what Ranieri and his innovation really did was fundamentally change the *ethic* of Wall Street from one where a buyer knew a seller, and vice versa, to one where the decision to buy something was separated from traditional market forces. No longer was a buyer making an affirmative decision to buy something from a seller he knew; now, in the hope of getting a big bonus, he was buying a slice of a package of stuff wrapped in a pretty bow that had the appearance of being worth what was advertised, but sometimes wasn't. Warren Buffett has referred to this phenomenon as the "three I's of new markets": the Innovators, the Imitators, and the Idiots, who end up taking a fine idea and pushing it to the brink of lunacy. "People don't get smarter about things that get as basic as greed," Buffett once said. "You can't stand to see your neighbor getting rich. You know you're smarter than he is, but he's doing all these [crazy] things, and he's getting rich . . . so pretty soon you start doing it."

Another Wall Street revolutionary was Michael Milken. Milken's innovation was to realize—as a graduate student at the Wharton School of Business in the 1970s—that investors could make more money, on a risk-adjusted basis, from buying the bonds issued by companies with less-than-stellar credit ratings than they could by investing in the bonds of AAA-rated companies. This has to do with the fact that not only do lower-rated bonds have more risk but also they pay their holders higher rates of interest. He realized that there was a very limited supply of such bonds, a supply that was unlikely to be able to meet investor demand once his discovery was out and fully appreciated. Armed with that extraordinary insight—which seems so obvious today but was anything but at the time—Milken and his firm, Drexel Burnham Lambert, a successor to the Drexel firm in Philadelphia that J. P. Morgan once controlled, set out to create a new supply of these so-called junk bonds by persuading companies that never before had access to the capital markets—where companies go to get capital from public investors as opposed to trying to get it from banks—to issue bonds underwritten by Drexel Burnham. Not only did Drexel underwrite these bonds for corporations that could not get financing from more traditional sources—banks, insurance companies, and the public-equity markets—but it also pioneered the selling of junk bonds to help corporate raiders, like Carl Icahn and T. Boone Pickens, get the capital they needed to take over companies such as TWA and Gulf Oil, which they would otherwise have been unable to do, and to help private-equity firms, such as Kohlberg Kravis Roberts and the Texas Pacific Group, get the money they needed to buy companies with their investors' money. Before long, the previously unknown firm of Drexel Burnham Lambert was both advising and financing these raiders and private-equity firms in their acquisition sprees. Drexel was reaping *huge* fees, and

Milken was getting rich beyond his wildest dreams. In 1987 alone, Drexel paid Milken *$550 million*. That's not a typo. But Milken was worth what he was being paid because Drexel was reaping billions of dollars in fees from his extraordinary innovation. Drexel dominated the junk-bond market for years before Milken's Wall Street brethren deconstructed what he was doing, copied him, and started competing with him.

During his Wall Street career (before he was banned from it for life), Milken financed more than thirty-two hundred companies across a wide swath of industries, household names that likely wouldn't have existed without the money he raised for them. Drexel's first junk-bond financing, in April 1977, was a $30 million bond for Texas International, a small oil-exploration company. Milken went on to finance Rupert Murdoch as he built News Corporation into an international powerhouse and Craig McCaw as he built a nationwide cellular communications company with two million subscribers before he sold it to AT&T for $11.5 billion, in 1994. He helped the billionaire entrepreneur John Malone build his cable-television empire and helped Bill McGowan create MCI, which competed against AT&T in the long-distance phone market. He helped to create Viacom, Time Warner Cable, Telemundo, and Metromedia. He helped finance KB Home, now the nation's largest home builder, as well as Toll Brothers Oriole Homes, and what is now Pulte. In the toy industry, Milken helped build Toys "R" Us, Mattel, and Hasbro. He financed Hilton, Days Inn, and Holiday Inn. In the gaming industry, he financed Mirage Resorts, Mandalay Resort Group, Harrah's, Park Place, and MGM, which together employ some 600,000 people. He helped build Safeway into a supermarket chain with nearly eighteen hundred stores and 200,000 employees. He financed 7-Eleven (Southland Corp.), Circle K, AMC Entertainment, Bally Manufacturing, Barnes & Noble, Beatrice, Caesars World, Calvin Klein, Chiquita Brands International, Danaher, Duracell, Filene's Basement, GAF Corporation, General Host Corporation, Kay Jewelers, Knoll International, Mellon Bank, Philadelphia Electric, Playtex, Sunshine Mining, and Uniroyal Goodrich. Countless other companies, financed by investment banks other than Drexel, probably wouldn't exist without the high-yield market that Milken created. It's not hyperbole to say that junk bonds underwritten by Wall Street firms have created millions of jobs that otherwise might not have existed, along with billions, if not trillions, of dollars in accumulated wealth.

Of course, nothing leads to excess like success. For years, Milken's power in the junk-bond market was near absolute. Unfortunately, he used it to line his own pockets at the expense of his clients and of his firm, Drexel

Burnham. He regularly siphoned off big fees for himself and would take the valuable equity positions in companies that he demanded in order to get deals done instead of passing them along to investors. In April 1990, after four years of investigation and prosecution, Milken agreed to plead guilty to six charges of criminal violation of securities laws—technical violations as opposed to the indictment that charged him with conspiracy and insider trading—and to pay a $600 million fine. He also paid another $500 million to Drexel's private investors who lost money when the firm was shuttered and then liquidated, also in 1990, as a result of Milken's wrongdoing. He denied any miscreant behavior for years before ultimately settling with federal prosecutors. He served twenty-two months in federal prison. But like parts of the securitization market, the junk-bond market continues to thrive to this day. It remains an incredibly important innovation, despite the hubris (and illegality) that Milken engaged in, and a source of huge annual profits for Wall Street.

In 2015 alone—thanks to Milken—nearly $372 billion was raised globally for companies with less-than-stellar credit ratings. The market—both new and existing issues—now totals some $2.2 trillion, tripling since 2005. In 2015, Valeant Pharmaceuticals raised $8.5 billion in the junk-bond market; Frontier Communications raised $6.6 billion; First Data raised $6.6 billion in two separate financings; Dollar Tree Inc. raised $3.25 billion; and Fiat Chrysler raised $3 billion. The money was used to build new factories, to buy new equipment, to create new products, and to hire more people and pay them decent wages. Why wouldn't we want to do everything we can to encourage the smooth operation of Milken's machine?

One of the final innovations to emerge from this period of remarkable financial alchemy came in 1994, at the still venerable, if not nearly so powerful as it once was, J.P. Morgan & Co. Exxon, a longtime client, wanted a $5 billion line of credit to cover potential liabilities related to the massive 1989 oil spill from the *Exxon Valdez* oil tanker in Prince William Sound, Alaska. The conundrum? The bank did not want to disappoint Exxon, but neither did it want to tie up so much capital in one marginally profitable, very risky loan. That's when the British-born Blythe Masters, then twenty-five years old, came up with the idea of off-loading the risk of the loan to a third party, in exchange for a fee, thus skirting the regulatory requirement that J.P. Morgan tie up capital against the risk posed by the Exxon loan. In short order, a new industry was born: the buying and selling of risk in what became known as "credit default swaps," a form of insurance policy that allowed creditors to buy insurance against the chance that a given loan or bond would default. But unlike a typical home insurance policy, which can be bought only by the owner of the home, or a life insurance policy, which can be bought only, generally speaking, by the person whose life is being insured, anyone could buy insurance against the risk that a loan, a bond, or some other kind of credit instrument might default. It was a form of legalized gambling. In exchange for annual premiums, anyone could bet that, say, a security that comprised a bunch of home mortgages might default on the mortgage payments, regardless of whether he or she owned the security or not. It was akin to allowing someone to bet whether your house would burn down. The anonymous person would pay annual premiums to an insurance company—money out the door every year— and the only way the bet would pay off would be if your house burned to the ground. Talk about a perverse set of incentives.

What could possibly go wrong?

The combination on Wall Street of a relative explosion of financial innovation, firms flush with new capital from outside investors, and a revamped incentive system that rewarded bankers, traders, and executives for the first time to take big risks with other people's money led quickly—and perhaps not unsurprisingly, especially in retrospect—to a rapid and virulent increase in the number and frequency of financial crises. Some of these crises were of Wall Street's making, some of them were not, and in some cases Wall Street threw gasoline on the pyre. Despite all the good things Wall Street had done for the American people, it couldn't help but get itself into trouble again and again.

Still, there was always an imperative among politicians and the American people to resolve and to move beyond the crises in order to get the economy percolating again. Wall Street simply had—and has—too important a role to play in the proper functioning of the American economy to have sand thrown in its gears. That doesn't mean that Wall Street does not often make it difficult for the American people to understand why it keeps causing trouble or why it should not be made less dangerous. But that is more a failure of public relations than anything else. The truth is that financial innovation is good for all of us. It leads to a lower cost of capital. It provides access to capital more broadly to more people when once upon a time capital was available only to the well heeled. It leads to most people being able to have their own credit card, or many of them—an unsecured line of credit that can be used to buy almost anything. It leads to most Americans being able to get a mortgage to buy a home, or a loan to buy a car or boat, or to borrow money to pay for a college education. It is also leading to a possible new revolution in finance—the so-called fintech industry—where the Internet supposedly eliminates the middlemen and matches investors directly with borrowers. Before the era of financial innovation, spurred on by the IPOs of Wall Street investment banks, it was not possible for an ordinary American to have a credit card or a low-priced mortgage or a car loan. The democratization of capital has led to more people in more places across the globe having the chance to pursue their dreams. Why in the world would we want to do anything to thwart them?

CHAPTER 8

Why Wall Street Matters

The 2008 bailouts of Wall Street left the American people fuming. But should they have been so upset? Would it have been better to have Wall Street collapse completely, with one leading firm after another cascading into bankruptcy and then somehow emerging in new forms, free from worthless assets and from financial obligations owed to others? It certainly would have purged—and potentially purified—the financial system, as does any baptism by fire. It's impossible, of course, to try to surmise what would have happened if the Federal Reserve and the Treasury had not bailed out Wall Street in 2008, because the Fed and the Treasury *did* bail out Wall Street in 2008. And by the way, though people may forget, that is *exactly* why the Federal Reserve was set up in the first place a century earlier: to bail out Wall Street if needed and to save capitalism from itself, the seeds of its own destruction having been sown from the start, as the economist Joseph Schumpeter famously argued.

Still, we fume. At the infamous April 2009 meeting in the Roosevelt Room at the White House between President Obama, then three months into the job, and the CEOs of the nation's biggest and most powerful banks, the mood was tense, to say the least. The stock market had hit its relative lows during the previous month. There was lots of noise about how Wall Street's just-bailed-out bankers had still managed to pay themselves multimillion-dollar bonuses. How could that have happened? Obama reportedly wanted to know. "These are complicated companies," one CEO said. Another added, "We're competing for talent on an international market." But the new president would have none of these justifications. "Be careful how you make those statements, gentlemen," Obama said. "The public isn't buying that." He added, "My administration is the only thing between you and the pitchforks." In a June 2009 interview with PBS, Ken Lewis, then the CEO of Bank of America, which had bought Merrill Lynch in the midst of the crisis and then paid its bankers big bonuses, said he understood why the American people were upset by the bonuses. "But it is disheartening, because what people are forgetting is that commercial banks are the very fabric of every community in which they operate," he said. He did not interpret Obama's "pitchfork" comment as a threat. Instead, he thought it was a turning point. "I interpreted it as kind of a watershed time, that we've been beaten up enough, that yeah, things have gone on that shouldn't have gone on and mistakes were made, but that banks are the catalyst to get us out of this recession, and that you can talk so long about the past, but at some point you've got to look at the present and the future," he said.

But if that meeting was a perceived turning point in the ongoing demonization of Wall Street for its role in fomenting the 2008 financial crisis, it was a premature one. Lewis resigned three months later. It was way too soon for the American people to want to forgive Wall Street. In September 2009, after a meeting in Pittsburgh of the G20, the leaders of the world's nineteen biggest economies plus the European Union issued a communiqué that essentially proclaimed that they would do everything in their power to prevent the big banks from ever again causing a financial crisis. Their public statement included the assertion that a new financial regulatory regime "for banks and other financial firms" needed to be put in place that "reins in the excesses that led to the crisis," adding that "where reckless behavior and a lack of responsibility led to crisis, we will not allow a return to banking as usual." The leaders "committed" to raising capital requirements for financial institutions and to "ending" compensation systems that "lead to excessive risk taking" and to holding bankers "to account" for the "risks" they are taking. "Standards for large global firms should be commensurate with cost of their failure." They added, for good measure, a thought that on its face is utterly contradictory: "We want growth without cycles of boom and bust and markets that foster responsibility not recklessness."

Once they committed to never having another financial crisis on their watch, and then directed their finance ministers and central bankers to make sure that happened, the inevitable result was to doom the largest economies of the world to a period of economic stagnation. The only way these leaders could think to restructure the banking industry to make sure that the big banks never again caused a financial crisis was to require that they massively increase the amount of capital they have on their balance sheets, to ensure there would be huge amounts of liquidity to absorb potential losses in the future value of assets on the books, a requirement that essentially stopped banks from taking anything that looked like a financial risk. Loans are inherently risky and require the belief that the bank will get paid back, but lending is also the lifeblood of capitalism, and to plant regulators in every bank to monitor closely what is going on and to veto anything that resembles wayward risk taking cuts off that bank's circulation. Suppressing the extension of credit to individuals and businesses not only fundamentally changes the nature of banks and banking but also creates a tremendous level of dissatisfaction among ordinary people who feel increasingly frustrated by their economic prospects, by the lack of growth in their wages, and by their inability to refinance their mortgages—or get a mortgage at all—or get a loan to buy a car or start a business. Feelings of economic hopelessness often lead to extreme voting patterns—witness the shocking rise of Trump and Sanders and the unexpected Brexit vote—and to political instability. The leaders of many of the countries at the G20 Summit in Pittsburgh sealed their own political fates by signing on to policies that pledged to radically alter the banking system, as a form of punishment for the bankers' bad behavior: Aside from Angela Merkel, the German president, they are mostly gone from office—including Nicolas Sarkozy in France and Gordon Brown in Great Britain—turned out by dissatisfied electorates. (Obama, of course, served out his two terms but President Trump seems determined to undo his legislative victories.)

In July 2010, the U.S. government followed through on the G20's pledge by passing the Dodd-Frank law, which included the Volcker Rule. Whereas the entire Glass-Steagall Act was a mere thirty-seven pages long, and the determinative sections that separated investment banking from commercial banking were about three of those pages, the Dodd-Frank law was some twenty-three hundred pages long. More than six years later, regulators and high-priced lawyers are still trying to figure out what it means.

It should be junked.

As should the Volcker Rule, which was the brainchild of Paul Volcker, the Fed chairman from 1979 until 1987 who tamed runaway inflation and who somehow decided that banks should no longer take risks with their capital because he thought that is what led to the 2008 financial crisis, even though it did not. (In fact, starting in December 2006 Goldman Sachs bet billions of its own money that trouble was brewing in the market for mortgage-related securities and made a fortune, bolstering the firm's financial prospects at the same time many of its competitors were going down the tubes.) Volcker's idea was to prevent Wall Street from ever again using its own capital to make proprietary bets, and he also wanted to limit the amount of its own money Wall Street could use to buy other companies as investments. The fact that neither of these behaviors had a hand in causing the 2008 financial crisis seemed not to occur to Paul Volcker. In

2010, Obama adopted Volcker's peculiar ideas about how to fix the banking system—no doubt in large part because they were consistent with the G20 dicta and because they must have seemed like good politics—and made them a central part of the Dodd-Frank legislation that he signed into law. Until it is somehow repealed, or revised—as Donald Trump has said he would do—the Dodd-Frank law condemns the banking sector to intense scrutiny, higher capital requirements, and an absolute aversion to risk taking. The new regulations have cleaned up certain excesses for now but have also made banks extremely reluctant to make loans. That may seem like the right way to curb the chance of another financial crisis, but it also, needlessly, condemns the economy to sluggishness, which makes it harder and harder for people to improve their economic standing and gives credence to the extraordinary statistic that some 46 percent of Americans surveyed told the Federal Reserve that they would be unable to write a $400 check in an emergency and instead would have to borrow from friends or put it on a credit card—a credit card they never would have had but for Wall Street.

There are other examples of dumb regulations that have been enacted in the wake of the 2008 financial crisis. For instance, the Federal Reserve has mandated that each "systematically important financial institution," what are known colloquially as the too-big-to-fail banks, be required to produce "living wills," hugely labor-intensive and costly documents that pretend to show what will happen the next time one of these banks gets into financial difficulty and how the Fed or the Treasury won't have to again intervene because it will all supposedly go down just as written on the living will. This false sense of security is, of course, beyond ridiculous, but for some bizarre reason the federal regulators take comfort in it. "The fact is that in most decisions, you don't go wrong with your logic," one Wall Street veteran told me in an interview. "You go wrong with your assumptions, and the assumption of where we are now is that we can control all things and nothing bad will ever happen." He, too, is skeptical of the living wills. With palpable sarcasm, he continued, "These institutions will just lay down and die in the right way? They'll go into a corner, and they'll go to sleep and they'll have an aneurysm and they'll die? They won't have an epileptic fit? They won't be thrashing around? They won't accidentally sort of hit somebody in the face and break their nose? They won't do that because they're going to do what we tell them, because we're going to keep the loans under very good control? We're going to do excellent analysis on it, and nothing will ever go in any direction that we mandate it won't? This is some kind of height of intellectual arrogance."

The Dodd-Frank law also requires big banks to undergo annual "stress tests" designed to gauge how they would fare in the face of another financial crisis. These tests are another colossal waste of time and money and, like the living wills, give regulators a false sense of security about what might happen during the next financial crisis. Bankers have tried to put the best face on this annual endurance test. *The Wall Street Journal* reported in June 2016:

Born of the financial meltdown in 2009, the stress tests have become a defining moment each year for big banks and investors. Bank executives manage their firms with one eye on how it will affect test results and have had to spend billions of dollars to develop systems to deal with them. They have become crucial for investors ever since the Fed decided in 2011 that the banks would have to submit capital-return plans as part of the tests and dividends and buybacks became dependent on the outcome of these hypothetical exercises. Some bankers have criticized the Fed's process as overly opaque and stringent and have complained that the higher capital required by them has choked lending and harmed the economy. That said, both bank executives and regulators have said the tests have made banks stronger and forced improvements in the ways that banks measure and manage risks.

It's clear that Washington's desire to punish Wall Street for the financial crisis has gone too far. Instead of facilitating the recovery of Main Street, Washington's policies have been thwarting it. Did you know that thanks to Washington's zealous compliance policies, the job of nearly one out of every five people working on Wall Street these days is to watch what the other four do all day long? Or that Washington's financial regulators can now freely attend meetings of a bank's board of directors? Or that bank regulators can now pass judgment on everything from the wisdom of an individual loan to how much capital a bank must have and how it uses it? Or that as a result of regulatory requirements, the bond market is now shockingly illiquid, costing millions of Americans with 401(k)s and pensions money every time they, or their fiduciaries, try to buy or sell a bond? Or that new regulations in the money-market industry have more than tripled the cost of the three-month London Interbank Offered Rate, or LIBOR, the short-term money rate that banks charge each other and on which most loans are based?

Have you tried to get a loan or a mortgage lately? It's not very easy, even for Ben Bernanke, the architect of the Fed's "zero-interest-rate policy" that has kept interest rates as low as they have ever been in our nation's history. In 2014, the newly private citizen Bernanke could not refinance the mortgage on his home because he no longer had a steady source of income. The additional irony of this anecdote is that despite the Fed's zero-interest-rate policies, it's nearly impossible for regular people to get their hands on it. What the government gives with one hand—virtually free money—it takes away with another, through new regulations that make actually getting any of that money harder than ever. If small and new businesses cannot borrow from banks, then job and wealth creation suffer mightily and economic growth stalls out.

Enough is enough. The ongoing vilification of Wall Street and the entire financial system has to stop. And it's not just Wall Street banks. We have to stop blaming banks of all stripes, many of which had nothing whatsoever to do with the financial crisis but are being victimized by the regulatory fallout from it anyway. According to Davis Polk, the Wall Street law firm, the new regulations governing the banking system run to more than 22,000 pages of new rules, on top of the 2,300 pages of the Dodd-Frank law—all of which is still in the process of being decoded, let alone understood, in the more than six years since the law was passed. Another 20 percent of the regulations mandated by Dodd-Frank still have not been written. According to Federal Financial Analytics Inc., the six largest U.S. banks by assets spent $70.2 billion in 2013 on regulatory compliance—nearly double what they collectively spent in 2007—and that is on top of the more than $200 billion in fines and penalties that federal and state prosecutors, as well as regulators, have extorted from shareholders of Wall Street banks for their role in causing the financial crisis. According to research done by IBM, more than twenty thousand new regulations were created in 2015 alone, and the "complete catalog" will exceed 300 million pages by 2020, "rapidly outstripping the capacity of humans to keep up." IBM estimated that complying with these regulations will soon cost financial institutions $270 billion a year. The new Trump administration has promised to reduce these burdensome regulations; let's hope it follows through on its promise.

It's not a matter of choice anymore; it's a matter of survival. The American banking system, once the envy of the world, must be allowed to succeed in its essential task of providing capital to those who need it to innovate, to start new businesses, to build new plants and equipment, and to hire employees at respectable wages. Washington cannot be allowed to prevail in its ongoing determination to make banks more like public utilities. Just because some 38,000 people were killed and another 4.4 million injured in automobile accidents in 2015, doesn't mean we ban cars. We try to make cars safer. The same principle must apply to banks. They must be allowed to take prudent risks and earn rewards for taking them. Prudent risk taking is essential to keeping our economy growing and innovating.

But at the moment, Washington is winning, and the American people are paying the heavy price for an economy that is mired in a low-growth, low-inflation, low-wage mode. Larry Summers, the Harvard economist and former Treasury secretary, refers to this lamentable state of affairs as the "secular stagnation" of an economy "stuck in neutral" and unable to generate annual GDP growth of more than 2 percent. "The reality is that if American growth continues to have a 2 per cent ceiling, it is doubtful that we will achieve any of our major national objectives," Summers wrote in an August 2016 *Washington Post* column. His consistent prescription has been the somewhat vague idea of creating "more demand for the product of business." (During the presidential campaign, Trump promised that his economic policies, including tax cuts, a $1 trillion infrastructure program, and less regulation, would result in annual GDP growth of 4 percent. Easier said than done.) In an October 2013 speech at Goldman Sachs—made public by a WikiLeaks hack into her campaign manager's e-mail account—Hillary Clinton seemed to share Summers's concerns about the dangers of the wrong kind of regulation in the banking sector. Of course, she didn't think what she said to Goldman Sachs would become public, even though she was paid $225,000 to answer questions for thirty minutes. But she showed she understood the important role Wall Street plays as the engine of our economy. She called Wall Street the country's "spinal column," and she is not wrong. "We need banking," she said. "Right now, there are so many places in our country where the banks are not doing what they need to do because they're scared of regulations, they're scared of the other shoe dropping, they're just plain scared, so credit is not flowing the way it needs to, to restart economic growth. They're still uncertain, and they're uncertain both because they don't know what might come next in terms of regulations, but they're also uncertain because of changes in a global economy that we're only beginning to take hold of." She said "first and foremost" there needs to be "more transparency" and "more openness" in the banking system in order to "keep this incredible economic engine in this country going."

Donald Trump has never spoken so precisely about his understanding of how Wall Street works, but surely he must have some inkling of it, given that his considerable fortune, whatever it is—he estimated it to be $11 billion—would not have been remotely possible without Wall Street. Whether he will remove the shackles that Dodd-

Frank has placed on the financial system, as he said he would, remains to be seen. In his first interview after winning the presidency on November 8, he told *The Wall Street Journal* that Dodd-Frank was "a tremendous burden to the banks." He added: "We have to get rid of it or make it smaller. . . . Banks are unable to lend. It's made our country noncompetitive. It's slowed down growth." He showed that he understands how the law is hurting the job-creating smaller businesses. "I can borrow money," he said. "The people who are really good, but need money to open a business or expand a business, can't borrow money from the banks." (Despite this statement, reforming Dodd-Frank has not made it on to the list of his top legislative priorities.) Steven Mnuchin, Trump's choice for Treasury secretary, said on CNBC on November 30 that Dodd-Frank is "way too complicated" and "cuts back lending." He said the administration's "number one priority on the regulatory side" would be to "strip back" parts of the law.

One of the best ways to get the economy growing again is to encourage banks to make loans, to take risks, to earn rewards, to innovate, and to provide liquidity to the capital markets. But those essential banking functions have been way off Washington's agenda. At the moment, Washington still wants banks to have higher capital requirements, to make fewer loans, to provide less liquidity to the capital markets, and to curtail innovation. The new regulations even dictate how a bank is allowed to advertise. And at the most extreme end, Senator Warren still wants to break up the big banks into little pieces and then she prays that those pieces dissolve. The problem on Wall Street is not the size of the banks, their concentration of assets, or the businesses they choose to be in. In fact, the big Wall Street banks are global leaders and the envy of competitors—especially in western Europe—that are struggling to figure out how to survive in a world of increasing regulation.

No, the problem on Wall Street remains one of improper incentives. When people are rewarded to take big risks with other people's money, that's exactly what they will do. The problem is that the top bankers, traders, and executives on Wall Street collectively no longer have enough of their own skin in the game to make a difference to them when the things they do go awry. They get rich either way. That is what needs to change on Wall Street, not some outdated, cockamamie notion of having the government dictate what businesses Wall Street can be in or how big a bank can be.

But politicians such as Senators Warren, Sanders, and McCain don't understand financial incentives or what motivates human behavior. (It's not clear that President Trump understands this, either.) They understand only political opportunism and getting reelected by currying populist favor. In fact, politicians and regulators remain intent on continuing to punish Wall Street for its role in causing the 2008 financial crisis and doing everything in their considerable power to make sure that Wall Street never blows up again. And while that might make sense if the banking system were a misbehaving child, the fact is that we need banks to take risks, we need them to make loans, we need them to make sure the capital markets have plenty of liquidity, and we need them to innovate and to come up with ways to make it possible for more people to have access to the capital they need at a low cost. Of course, as part of these essential functions, bankers, traders, and executives also must be held accountable for their bad behavior. But that is a task for the Justice Department, not politicians and regulators looking to vilify an entire group of hardworking people. Sanders and Warren have gone so far as to prevent people with Wall Street experience from serving in government, especially at its highest levels. They have reiterated they will continue to try to block Trump's nominations if the nominees worked on Wall Street. (Trump seems indifferent to their threats and has loaded his administration with Wall Street types, despite the fact that Wall Street had long before stopped financing his business schemes.)

But instead of allowing banks to do what banks do,

Washington would prefer to paralyze them from the neck down, using the 2010 Dodd-Frank law and its Volcker Rule as their principal cudgels. (And of course, for reasons already discussed, Senator Warren's 21st Century Glass-Steagall Act, if it were ever to get political traction and become law, which seems highly unlikely, would do that in spades, too.) The new regulations have hit community banks—those with less than $10 billion in assets— especially hard. Marshall Lux and Robert Greene, at Harvard's Kennedy School of Government, found that while community banks accounted for 22 percent of outstanding bank loans, they accounted for more than 75 percent of agricultural loans and half of small business loans, but they also found that the number of community banks fell 14 percent between 2010, when the Dodd-Frank law was passed, and 2014.

Just when growing income inequality has made the need for lending to small and local businesses an imperative, community banks are playing less of a role than they had previously in extending credit, in taking deposits, and in facilitating commerce. Most top bank executives are terrified to speak out about this situation, for the obvious reason that federal and state regulators control their bank charters. But Robert Wilmers, the CEO of Buffalo's fast-growing M&T Bank, is not afraid. "A restoration of those crucial roles will require a healthier dialogue between bankers and regulators, an appreciation of the unintended consequences of new policies, a grasp of the implications of technological change, and an understanding of the rapidly evolving financial services industry as a whole," he wrote to his shareholders in 2016. "Though small and mid-sized banks played little, if any, role in the crisis, they have been swept into this vast change, and the resulting disproportionate burden is distracting them from their traditional focus on servicing local families, businesses and farmers. Despite a shared objective of maintaining the safety and soundness of the financial system, today's banking environment is typified by a relationship between institutions and governing agencies that is less than collaborative—a product, it seems, of a political atmosphere where pressure remains upon banks to prove themselves reformed."

Regulators and central bankers are also taking their toll on the big Wall Street banks that have historically made sure the capital markets function properly. Compliance officers are everywhere these days. JPMorgan Chase hired 8,000 compliance officers in 2015; out of a workforce of 236,000, 43,000 are now involved in compliance functions, nearly double the number from 2011. Goldman Sachs increased its employee count in 2015, to 36,800, many of whom it has said were compliance officers. Regulators are everywhere, too. Whereas before the financial crisis it was rare for a Washington regulator to make an appearance inside a Wall Street bank—the so-called light-touch approach—now "people are seeing regulators constantly," one Wall Street senior executive told me.

Since Morgan Stanley became a bank holding company in the midst of the financial crisis, regulators are crawling all over the place. On-site federal examiners from both the Federal Reserve and the Office of the Comptroller of the Currency have their own offices at Morgan Stanley. "They can go wherever they want whenever they want," explained Ruth Porat, the former Morgan Stanley chief financial officer, in an interview before she took the same job at Google. They can go to board meetings. They can look at and monitor the loan portfolio. They examine every leveraged loan. They are looking at credit decisions regularly. She tried to put the best face on the new reality. "It's made us a better firm," she said. "It's made us more predictable." Jamie Dimon, the chairman and CEO of JPMorgan Chase, is far less diplomatic. He said Wall Street is "under assault" from regulators. "In the old days, you dealt with one regulator," he said in a conversation with investors. "Now it's five or six. You all should ask the question how American that is."

New regulations are also rapidly curtailing what was once an essential function of Wall Street: to provide liquidity to the bond market, making it possible for clients, big and small, to sell their bonds at a favorable price without dramatically moving the market price up or down. In other words, it was the way you could be pretty sure that when you sold your Johnson & Johnson bond when it was trading at a hundred cents on the dollar, you received a hundred cents on the dollar for it. Now Wall Street is abandoning that business, in the wake of regulators' forcing Wall Street banks to allocate more of their precious capital against securities warehoused on their balance sheets. Instead of tying up capital this way, Wall Street is increasingly no longer making those markets. This may seem like an esoteric, irrelevant development. But it's not. Anyone who owns bonds in a brokerage account, in a 401(k), or in a pension fund—in other words, more than 100 million Americans—will now have a much more difficult time selling a bond at a price he or she finds acceptable. That will hurt. The pain became apparent in the wake of Trump's victory, when the bond market had a dramatic selloff, in part because of this decreased liquidity.

Then there is the recent saga of the short-term interest rate known as LIBOR. Should you care? Definitely. LIBOR is the rate used to price nearly every loan around the world. It is also the rate that banks use to lend each other money. In the last year or so, the cost of three-month LIBOR has more than tripled in price (to one hundred and two basis points, from thirty-two basis points) with hardly anyone taking notice. The rapid move upward in LIBOR came in reaction to new SEC regulations that went into effect in October 2016 in the money-market fund industry, as well as to other changes in how banks are regulated that were expected to take effect in December 2016 and January 2017. Banks are starting to charge each other much more for short-term loans, which is an ominous sign, and stands in stark contrast to the new highs being achieved in the stock market and the rally in Treasury securities (before it sold off dramatically in the wake of Trump's unexpected victory).

The SEC's new rules for money-market funds require that they represent to investors that the funds are "money good," or worth what they say they are worth. The problem being addressed by the SEC, at the instigation of the Federal Reserve, occurred in September 2008 when the Reserve Fund, a money-market fund—which is supposed to be as safe as a savings account—"broke the buck," meaning that $1 invested in the fund, which was supposed to always be worth $1, was no longer worth $1. It was a traumatic moment of the crisis. People lost money on what was supposed to be a safe investment. They were upset, of course. But more important to the confidence of the financial system was the fact that because of the turmoil in the markets, a money-market fund was no longer considered prudent. The reason the Reserve Fund "broke the buck" is that it didn't just keep the money investors gave it in cash; it invested the money, in an effort to give investors a slightly higher yield, or financial return on the money invested, than could be found in a savings account. The Reserve Fund generated those slightly higher returns by investing in something that seemed to be rated AAA—the AAA tranches of securitizations, the funky and creative securities created by Lew Ranieri—that turned out not to be really AAA after all (as we all know). Understandably, the Federal Reserve doesn't want that to happen again, hence the new rules about money-market funds that took effect last year. The problem, as usual, is not the honorable goal of trying to prevent a money-market fund from ever again breaking the buck; the problem is the unintended consequences of trying to make sure that doesn't happen.

Once upon a time, Alan Greenspan, another former Federal Reserve Board chairman, spoke about the Fed's being an organization that set monetary policy with a minor regulatory function attached to it. Today, the Fed's monetary function is the minor appendage to its growing regulatory juggernaut. One man, Daniel Tarullo, has become the embodiment of the Fed's new focus; in the process, he has become the most feared and powerful

Washington banking regulator. He is also unknown to the American people. (That needs to change; a bright light needs to be focused on him and his reforms.) Tarullo is the driving force at the Fed seeking to make sure things like "breaking the buck" never happen again. Tarullo has the power to make that happen, because he is in charge of regulating the big banks as chairman of the Federal Financial Institutions Examination Council (a mouthful for sure). But Tarullo's mission also shows how far regulators are going these days to eliminate risk inside Wall Street's biggest banks, and that will have unintended consequences—like higher rates for borrowed money—for the rest of us.

Obama appointed Tarullo to the Federal Reserve's board of governors in January 2009. (His term expires in January 2022, although in the wake of Trump's election there have been rumors that he might leave Washington before then.) A graduate of Georgetown, Duke, and Michigan Law School, Tarullo, born in Boston, has taught at Harvard Law School, has worked in the Justice Department and the Commerce Department, and has served as a member of the National Economic Council and the National Security Council. He also was an assistant secretary of state in the Clinton administration. He is a fan of the Red Sox, *Seinfeld*, and William Faulkner. He has been described as the "Wizard of Oz" for the power he wields behind the scenes. *The Wall Street Journal* has called Tarullo the "most important person in the banking business" for the sway he holds over banks. He has administered the so-called stress tests—the complicated annual computer modeling exercises that banks are forced to do in order to hypothesize what might happen during a future financial crisis. They're pointless war games for Wall Street, and they cost banks hundreds of millions of dollars to comply with. Tarullo also uses them to determine whether Wall Street banks can pay dividends to their shareholders.

Tarullo began to grab the reins of power at the Federal Reserve in 2010, in the wake of the financial crisis, when he took over the important responsibility of regulating the big Wall Street banks from the Federal Reserve Bank of New York. "It was obvious that a lot in the U.S. regulatory system had not worked particularly well before the crisis," Tarullo told *The Wall Street Journal* in 2010. "It was equally obvious that there was going to need to be a rethink and reorganization." (Such is the secrecy surrounding the Fed's various moves that Tarullo's takeover of the regulation of Wall Street from the Federal Reserve Bank of New York went unreported for five years until *The Wall Street Journal* obtained a copy of the so-called Triangle Document that described the changes.) Shifting the regulatory control of Wall Street to Washington, from

New York, is significant but subtle given the long-standing power the Federal Reserve Bank of New York had always had. For close to a hundred years, the New York Fed's proximity to Wall Street was seen as an asset. After the financial crisis, that closeness became a liability. "This reserve bank doesn't breathe any more without asking Washington if it can inhale or exhale," a prominent New York banker told the *Journal* of the New York Fed.

Tarullo has slowly but surely started to dismantle many pieces of the financial system that have come to define Wall Street in the last forty-five years, as one firm after another flocked to the public markets as a source of abundant, cheap capital and began to use that cheap money from other people to innovate and to take bigger and bigger risks. Tarullo seems particularly keen to make sure that risk taking by banks is curtailed. But he is working subtly. He attracts few headlines and makes fewer proclamations. He has adopted Fed-speak as his native tongue, making his Delphic pronouncements difficult to decipher for those not paying close attention. But he is forcing real change on Wall Street.

For instance, he has demanded that banks raise much more capital. Between early 2009 and the third quarter of 2014, the capital at the nation's fifty largest banks has increased to $1.2 trillion, from $506 billion. He also seems determined to kill off the securitization market, which packages up streams of home-mortgage payments, car payments, and credit-card payments and sells them off as securities. He correctly blames Wall Street for the excesses in the mortgage-securitization market that helped exacerbate the 2008 financial crisis. Does that mean that much of the securitization market should also be wiped out as a consequence, despite the benefit of lower rates and access to capital that the market has provided to the average American? Obviously not.

But Tarullo is on a mission. In a July 2016 speech, he spoke of the risk of "runnable liabilities," by which he meant essentially what happened in 2008 when short-term secured lenders decided to no longer lend to the Wall Street firms because they no longer trusted the value of the collateral that secured those loans. The short-term loans ran away, he's right to point out, leaving Bear Stearns, Merrill Lynch, Lehman Brothers, and Morgan Stanley, among others, without enough liquidity to operate their businesses. Chaos ensued. "As has been frequently observed, the recent financial crisis began, like most banking crises, with a run on short-term liabilities by investors who had come to doubt the value of the assets they were funding through various kinds of financial intermediaries," he said in his July 2016 speech. He noted correctly that unlike the bank runs that typified the

1930s, when small depositors lined up to get their money out, in 2008 it was the institutions that ran for the exits without having to line up at all. They got out simply by—literally—pushing a button on their computers. What happened next, Tarullo explained, was that the Wall Street banks, "lacking enough liquidity to repay all the counterparties who declined to roll over their investments," were forced "into fire sales that further depressed asset prices, thereby reducing the values of assets held by many other intermediaries, raising margin calls, and leading to still more asset sales." Better-capitalized firms, he continued, tended "to hoard" their financial resources "in light of their uncertainty as to whether their balance sheets might come under greater stress and their reluctance to catch the proverbial falling knife by purchasing assets whose prices were plummeting with no obvious floor."

Tarullo's postcrisis effort to "protect financial stability" remains focused on regulating "runnable securities." Hence his mandate that money-market funds, in which millions of Americans park billions of their dollars believing them to be safe and secured, could no longer invest in the AAA tranche of securitizations. In Tarullo's world, they were no longer considered "safe" investments. Preventing money-market funds from investing in the top tranche of securitizations will definitely make them safer, especially as the funds replace these purchases with those of genuinely safer Treasury securities. The unintended consequence of Tarullo's decision, though, is to stick a dagger in the heart of the securitization market because a key buyer of the top tranche of the securities has been regulated away and without that buyer, the market fades. In the first half of 2016, the issuance of asset-backed securities by Wall Street banks—outside of those backed by the government-controlled entities Fannie Mae and Freddie Mac—fell 36 percent from the same period the previous year. The issuance of mortgage-backed securities fell 42 percent in the same period.

Needless to say, Tarullo is detested on Wall Street. One Wall Street CEO told me Tarullo was "like a law unto himself." He said that "everybody in the business completely hates" Tarullo. "He doesn't care what the fuck happens to the economy," he continued. "He's just in his own little zone. People live in fear of this guy because they can't negotiate with him. He's like a dictator and only he knows what is right."

A few people have an understanding of what Tarullo is doing, and have written about it, with some considerable passion. "All of this essentially comes down to the FED moving decisively AND OUT OF NECESSITY to literally take back the definition of MONEY from the Wall Street firms that have spent the better part of the last 30 years re-defining it on their own terms, and for their own convenience," Ralph Del Guidice, the cofounder of Madrone Macro-Economic Advisors, wrote to his clients in August 2016. (Emphasis his.) ". . . Get ready for a repricing across the board, because that is going to be the ugly result here AND AS FAR AS THE FED IS CONCERNED; C'est La Vie . . . If you take away the financial alchemy and let markets be markets don't be surprised at the outcome."

John Fichthorn, a hedge fund manager at Dialectic Capital Management, has carefully studied Tarullo's moves to redesign the financial system and has used his hedge fund to figure out a way to benefit should the markets blow up again as a result. It's the kind of swing-for-the-fences bet that a small group of hedge fund managers—who were memorialized in Michael Lewis's best-selling book *The Big Short* and in Adam McKay's 2015 film of the same name—made in the years leading up to the 2008 financial crisis. Fichthorn has set up his own big short because he thinks Tarullo's zealousness will lead the economy off a cliff. He told me that Tarullo and the other regulators at the Fed share a maniacal belief that the financial system would not have survived the 2008 financial crisis without a federal bailout. "Now I think that's a bunch of shit," he said. "They think every failure must be bailed out because they think every failure has the risk of spreading, causing market volatility, and lower asset prices equals fewer jobs—and whatever else goes into their thinking. They don't like the fact that they feel like they have to bail out the system every five years."

Fichthorn would prefer to believe that the market, as it has done for generations, will sort the winners from the losers and there is no need for the federal government to assume that it must always bail out the bad boys on Wall Street because that leads to the view that risk taking on Wall Street has to be curtailed to prevent bad behavior. He believes that even in turbulent markets, there will always be people willing to invest capital for the higher returns commensurate with the risks involved. In other words, Fichthorn wants the regulators to let the market work. "That's not their belief," he told me. "Their belief is they have to save it. They have to save it once every five years. So how do we get rid of what we have to save? Well, it's not our fault because we save it every time and make the problem bigger. It's their fault because they created securitizations. And it's not that securitizations aren't a problem, but, frankly, if they let the market work itself out, the market would get rid of the securitizations that didn't work. But they don't do that. They always have to save it."

He said he thinks the unintended consequence of Tarullo's "jihad"—his word, not mine—is to curb what has made Wall Street the envy of the world: risk taking, innovation, and entrepreneurship. He imagines that the Fed governors are sitting around their big oval table in Washington, scratching their heads, wondering why there's less job creation than there should be, why there are fewer small businesses being started, why there is a decrease in entrepreneurial behavior, why the economy's growth remains so sluggish. "The answer is because without creative destruction you don't have new business formation, and they have decided creative destruction is not what they like," he said. "They don't like anything that has the word 'destruction.' So they stopped the destruction, and therefore there was no creative creation that followed it." He can't do anything to influence Tarullo or the Fed, of course, so he is doing the only thing he can do given his view that Tarullo's strategy will end badly, very badly: He has made a big bet against the American economy so that he and his investors can benefit if he's right.

Tarullo is determined to eliminate Wall Street's financial alchemy, and in doing so, he hopes to make markets safer and to prevent a recurrence of the continuous stream of financial rescues that have plagued Wall Street since 1987. Nor is Tarullo a lone wolf at the Fed. In November 2016—eight days *after* Donald Trump was elected president of the United States, Neel Kashkari, the president of the Federal Reserve Bank of Minneapolis (and it's worth noting, a former Goldman Sachs banker and TARP regulator), has created what he is calling the "Minneapolis Plan," a demand that big-bank capital be increased beyond what even Tarullo has required. Kashkari has in mind breaking up the big banks by requiring that they hold so much capital that it no longer makes sense to keep them together. This is just more regulatory foolishness.

In sum, the Fed has decided in its infinite wisdom that preventing Wall Street from ever again causing a financial crisis is more important than allowing Wall Street to innovate and to do what it does best: to provide the much-needed capital to businesses the world over that need it. (Neither Tarullo nor Kashkari responded to requests to be interviewed.) That's fine if the American people still believe that punishing Wall Street will somehow benefit them. The reality is far different: The sooner Wall Street and community banks are permitted to return to their traditional role of taking capital from those who have it and providing it to those who want and need it, free from onerous, punitive regulations, the sooner the power of the American economy will again be unleashed. Until then, our economy will indeed be stuck in neutral. Worse, Larry Summers told *The Wall Street Journal* in August

2016, when the next recession inevitably hits, the Fed will have fewer ways to get us out of it, given how low it has deliberately kept interest rates since 2008. "We should be extremely worried," Summers said. "We are essentially on a fairly dangerous battlefield with very little ammunition."

What we need on Wall Street is smart regulation, not political, retaliatory regulation. What Tarullo is doing in trying to prevent another financial crisis is unwinding decades of financial innovations that have actually benefited the American people by allowing them access to capital at lower prices than would otherwise have been possible. Tarullo is no doubt sincere in his mission to make financial markets safer, but at what cost? We need a way to reward bankers, traders, and executives for taking prudent financial risks and developing new financial innovations while also holding them accountable for their bad behavior. The days of socializing the risks and privatizing the gains, which should have come to an end after the 2008 financial crisis, have to be stopped. In the eight years since the most acute part of the financial crisis, there has been nary a word about revamping Wall Street's asymmetric compensation system. Incredibly, despite the compensation system's role in rewarding bankers, traders, and executives with big bonuses for taking risks with other people's money, they still get rewarded to take big risks with other people's money, and there's only a superficial effort—at best—to hold them accountable when things go wrong. Sure, there is talk of "clawing back" bonuses from people who misbehave, but I can't think of a single example—except for the recent debacle involving Wells Fargo—where this has actually happened. What is more prevalent, by far, is that people on Wall Street still get rewarded with multimillion-dollar bonuses and promotions for their bad behavior.

My favorite example of this egregious, and ongoing, behavior is David Miller, a managing director at Credit Suisse. In March 2016, in an effort to right the ship on the credit side of the investment bank, Credit Suisse named Brian Chin, the chief of structured finance, and Miller, the chief of credit products, to be co-chiefs of the bank's global markets credit division. This was yet another big job for Miller, with lots of responsibility and high pay, but his appointment sends exactly the wrong message about the values and behavior that a Wall Street bank should be rewarding. Miller was the bank's architect, starting in 2004, of a new syndicated loan product— called a dividend recapitalization loan—that allowed big-time real-estate developers in the western half of the United States to borrow lots of money based on the inflated valuation of their projects, pocket hundreds of millions of dollars in the form of dividends, and lay the risk at the doorstep of new investors whom Miller and his team had lined up.

From 2004 to 2006, Miller and Credit Suisse arranged for $5 billion of these kinds of loans, which were then sold to investors. The deals produced hundreds of millions of dollars in fees for the bank, a high percentage of which, of course, went into the pockets of Miller and his team. From 2004 to 2008, Miller received compensation of $23.1 million, including $7.2 million in 2006 alone. In the end, all of the loans—every single one—blew up, and investors lost billions. After each of the developments ended up in bankruptcy court, a federal bankruptcy judge admonished the Credit Suisse bankers by calling the loans "doomed to failure" from the outset.

An affiliate of Highland Capital Management, a hedge fund based in Dallas that was a creditor in some of these projects, argued in a lawsuit that "Credit Suisse was motivated by naked greed in perpetrating its fraudulent scheme."

E-mails released as part of the litigation give a glimpse of the type of culture that Miller fostered in his group and its obvious lack of accountability. In an internal September 2004 e-mail to other Credit Suisse executives, Miller promoted the soon-to-close Lake Las Vegas deal—the bank's first "dividend recapitalization loan." He bragged about how the development's half owners, the wealthy Bass brothers of Texas, were going to get what turned out to be a $469 million dividend. Fellow Credit Suisse bankers marveled at the deal's ingenuity for creating new business seemingly out of nowhere. "You must have the biggest and deepest dredge known to mankind," Grant Pothast, then head of the bank's distressed-loan group, wrote to Miller. Responded Miller, "I go wherever I can find a fee," while noting that the bank would be making $9 million on the deal. He added that he took comfort in knowing that his colleagues were willing "to work in the deep dredges of life with me." After the deal closed in November 2004, it was hailed internally as "a tremendous success."

According to e-mails disclosed as part of the lawsuits, Miller was singled out for bringing "creativity on structure," "thoughtful advice on positioning," and "calm, assuring feedback to the client," and for "pushing the real estate bankers to roll this out to other homebuilders." As the machine got cranking in August 2005, and after one of Miller's colleagues questioned an aspect of the creative structure, Miller replied, "These are aggressive deals and it is in all of our best interests that the investors are protected, because if one of them blows up, you will see these investors pull out of this land development mkt [market] and our gravy train will stop." After the Lake Las Vegas deal was refinanced in June 2007, based on what turned out to be overinflated appraisals of the value of the property, a news article about the deal was circulated internally at Credit Suisse. "This reads like we operate some sort of gene splicing lab—or a bell and whistle factory," Tom Newberry, the chief of the bank's syndicated loan group, wrote to Miller and others, according to an e-mail contained in the court filings. You would think Newberry might be questioning the morality or ethics of making these kinds of loans. Wrong. "Congratulations," he wrote.

"We are going to start recruiting Physics PhD's from MIT," Miller replied.

"We don't need them," wrote Newberry. "Dr. Frankenstein is apparently already an employee."

Credit Suisse, of course, stands by its man and refuses to acknowledge how unfortunate it is for the credibility of Wall Street for bankers such as Miller to still be employed, let alone to be promoted and rewarded lavishly. Frankly, it's gross. The bank "has a zero-tolerance policy which we take very seriously," Nicole Sharp, a company spokeswoman, wrote to me in an e-mail. "Our conduct and integrity is of utmost importance to how we operate. These are old matters which continue to be litigated and we do not wish to comment." Of course not.

Nor is a simple clawback of an employee's bonus—

even though it never seems to happen—or that an employee gets some of his or her compensation in deferred stock a sufficient deterrent for bad behavior. Jimmy Cayne, the former chairman and CEO of Bear Stearns, at one time had a net worth of $1.6 billion, about $1 billion of which was in his firm's stock. He was the first Wall Street CEO to hold more than $1 billion of his firm's stock. And when Bear's stock hit its all-time high in January 2007, Cayne no doubt felt like the happiest man on Wall Street. You would have thought that because he had more than 60 percent of his net worth tied up in Bear Stearns stock, he would have been deeply focused on the firm and the risks that were accruing there. In the end, having more than $1 billion tied up in Bear's stock was not enough to keep his eye on the ball. Perhaps he just didn't understand the risks that had built up in his firm, or perhaps he was more interested in playing bridge—he is an aficionado—or in smoking marijuana, one of his bad habits, to stay focused—or maybe it was a combination of all three. During an interview I did with him for *House of Cards,* my 2009 book about the demise of Bear Stearns, he told me about first coming to grips with the fact that JPMorgan Chase was thinking of buying Bear Stearns at a deep discount to its then trading price. He had arrived in New York at around 6:00 P.M. on the Saturday of the firm's fateful March 2008 weekend from Detroit, where he had been playing in a bridge tournament. At this time, Cayne was no longer the firm's CEO, but he was still the board chairman. He heard the news about the value of the proposed deal and started doing the math. "I'm saying to myself [I've got] six million shares, I just got my ass kicked," he told me in 2008. "But I was almost dispassionate, because to me, $8 and $12 were the same. It was not $170, and it wasn't $100. And it wasn't $40. The only people [who] are going to suffer are my heirs, not me. Because when you have a billion six and you lose a billion, you're not exactly like crippled, right?"

Exactly right. Someone who still has $600 million in cash lying around is unlikely to be nearly as upset as someone who had nothing remaining of a $1.6 billion fortune. It's like the difference between a chicken and a pig in a ham and egg breakfast: The chicken is interested; the pig is committed. The leaders of Wall Street's banks need to be totally committed to their firms, not just merely interested.

We need to eliminate the bonus culture on Wall Street and return to a compensation system that more closely resembles that of the partnership culture from the years before DLJ filed its IPO in 1969. It wouldn't be hard to do, either. It just requires the leadership of a Wall Street firm to want to make the change. Unfortunately, gutsy leadership is in short supply on Wall Street these days.

And while Senator Warren won't like to hear this, "bigger" is not an inherently bad thing to be when it comes to finance. In any event, there would be major impediments, of course, to returning the big Wall Street banking behemoths to the small, undercapitalized partnerships that they once were, and not just because I don't like Senator Warren's idea of breaking up the big banks. Making Goldman Sachs or JPMorgan Chase private partnerships again would mean, essentially, buying out the public shareholders. The market value of Goldman's equity these days is around $100 billion, before a takeover premium is added; JPMorgan Chase is even bigger, with an equity value of around $300 billion. That's before including the billions more in debt that these two companies owe that would likely have to be refinanced as part of any going-private transaction. There probably isn't enough risk capital around to take Goldman Sachs or Morgan Stanley or JPMorgan Chase private and substitute private investors' capital for that of the public. Nor would we even want that. It wouldn't fix the problem. What we need to fix the problems on Wall Street is a dramatic change in the compensation and incentive structure. And we need it now.

But we can aspire to a compensation system that more closely resembles what used to happen in private partnerships when it came to accountability. Once upon a time on Wall Street, the partners at these firms had their entire net worth on the line if something went wrong. That's why Wall Street was often such a dangerous place for so many Wall Street banks and their partners. One slipup, and all was lost, especially in the days before the federal government rescued Bear Stearns from bankruptcy and there was no hope of a public-sector rescue for a Wall Street firm. If the partnership folded, individual partners likely lost every asset they had accumulated in their lives as creditors swarmed over a firm's carcass.

That's the prescription for what ails Wall Street: The leaders of the big Wall Street firms once again need to have their full net worth on the line if something starts going wrong at their firms. They need to know that everything they built up over the years—their Fifth Avenue co-op, their house in the Hamptons, their art collection, their bank account—will be fodder for the bank's creditors.

What needs to happen—and fast—is that the leaders of the remaining big Wall Street firms need to designate the top five hundred or so top executives at their respective firms—the ones that run business lines, decide how capital gets allocated, decide who gets how much compensation and who gets promoted and who doesn't—and along with the other members of the executive suite create a way for the bank's creditors and shareholders to be able to go after their full net worth—everything—in the case of a meltdown, akin to what happened at Bear Stearns, Merrill Lynch, and Lehman Brothers and what was certainly on the verge of happening at Morgan Stanley.

The leaders of Wall Street need some serious incentive to behave properly and to no longer take imprudent risks with other people's money. This suggestion is meant not as punishment but as a fundamental acknowledgment of human nature, whether there is a Wall Street or not. Remember, people are pretty simple. They do what they are rewarded to do. In the years leading up to the 2008 financial crisis, they were rewarded to manufacture shoddy mortgages, package them up into securities, get them a phony AAA credit rating, and sell them off around the world as supposedly legitimate investments. In 2016, eight years after the second-worst financial crisis in our history, bankers, traders, and executives are still being rewarded to take big risks with other people's money. Unless and until that reward system changes—and no one seems to be even remotely talking about changing it—we cannot expect Wall Street's bankers, traders, and executives to change their behavior.

This one simple change in the Wall Street compensation system would render Dodd-Frank and the Volcker Rule irrelevant. They both could be torn up and thrown in the trash. The compliance culture could be rolled back considerably. Elizabeth Warren could stop her inane push for some kind of new Glass-Steagall Act, which has absolutely no relevance anymore. The government could get out of the business of forcing Wall Street to turn into utilities, where every move has to be watched and monitored. When the top bankers, traders, and executives on Wall Street once again have their full net worth on the line—not a portion of it, but *all* of it—then we can rest assured they will start doing the right things. That's smart regulation, and not a sole person is even considering it. In the meantime, we have incredibly dumb regulation.

Economic growth is nearly perfectly correlated with the extension of credit. But when banks are being encouraged not to extend credit, or the price they have to pay for extending credit—on both the financial and the regulatory fronts—encourages them not to do so, then the economies of the world are condemned to zero growth, and that is basically what is happening in the United States, western Europe, and Japan, three of the world's four largest economies. The whole world is struggling to get economic growth. "The reason that that's happened isn't because we had a financial crisis," one senior Wall Street executive told me. "It's because the way we decided to reform from this financial crisis created the shortage of capital and led to financial repression. It's made it impossible for financial intermediaries to perform their normal role because we have regulators who are acting on behalf of legislatures and presidents and prime ministers of countries to get the financial institutions into such a position of liquidity and lack of ability to lend that it just made it difficult to start new businesses and to expand in a normal way."

He said the Obama administration's philosophy about banking regulations and the proper way banks should behave—essentially more like utilities—has been "the straw that's breaking the camel's back" and is condemning the nation's economy to years of slow growth. He said these regulators, operating with the new philosophical outlook, are "not connected" to the "societal implications of what they're doing" and believe they are just "mechanics who need to screw down the system." He said the decisions that have ended up curtailing the issuance of credit are "acts of relative insanity."

He agreed that junking parts of the Dodd-Frank law and the entire Volcker Rule would be the right place to start on the path to smarter regulation. He said that if six years after the passage of the Dodd-Frank law many of its required regulations still had not been written, "doesn't that tell you that the law makes no sense?" He said he'd streamline it considerably: Keep the regulations that work and make sense and eliminate the rest. He suggested he'd fire all the regulators and start again with a new group of people. He proposed seconding to the agencies that regulate Wall Street groups of relatively senior bankers and traders—fifth- or sixth-year professionals—for a year to essentially teach the regulators whatever the latest tricks of the trade are on Wall Street. The plan would be not only to make the regulators smarter about what Wall Street is up to but also to make their proposed regulations more targeted and more meaningful. Plus it would give the future leaders of Wall Street a better understanding of the mindset of their regulators, creating the possibility of having meaningful conversations if needed by adversaries with some personal relationships. "They can learn what's actually going on in these financial institutions as opposed to just getting reports," he said. "That way, you'd also be training the next cadre of leadership in the financial institutions to learn what the concerns are, and you would have a melding of knowledge and practice."

He said it is essential that people know the truth about what happened in September 2008 when the Federal Reserve, the Treasury, and Congress worked together to save Wall Street and not some mythologized version of it. "Yes, there were excesses," he said, explaining how the story should go, "but here's what happened." The Federal Reserve, working together with the Treasury and Congress, did in 2008 what J. P. Morgan did in 1907 and what could not be done by any individual banker ever again. The system had become too big and too interconnected for that. The Federal Reserve did what it was created to do, as the lender of last resort. Short-term, secured loans were made to a variety of financial institutions, large and small, using unencumbered assets at the banks as collateral for the loans. As part of the cash infusions, the government took warrants in these banks and financial institutions. The loans to the banks were paid back in full and the warrants had tremendous value. The government made a profit of $15.3 billion. "It's probably the only government program in history where it actually made a profit," he said.

There have been times during the history of the human race when people become delusional. Even though things are obviously wrong, people living at the time believe they are right. They become convinced something is an absolute truth, even though it is not, and it seems that nothing is able to dissuade them from their belief until reality finally sets in, often years later. People believed the world was flat. They believed the sun revolved around the Earth. They did not believe in evolution. They believed putting leeches on their bodies cured disease. And on and on.

Continuing to demonize Wall Street more than eight years after the financial crisis and to prevent it from doing what Wall Street does better than any financial system on the face of the planet—allocate capital from those who have it and provide it efficiently to those who want it—has gone far beyond punishment for Wall Street. The policies of the Washington regulators are now punishing the American people and condemning our economy to slow and desultory growth.

The fix for Wall Street should be directed at its compensation system, not at the functioning of Wall Street itself. It's really as simple as that. Fix the compensation system—make bankers, traders, and executives fear for their art collections, their co-ops, and their homes in the Hamptons—and sit back and watch how quickly it works to change people's bad behavior.

And forget what the ongoing demonization means for Wall Street bankers, traders, and executives. They don't need sympathy. Much more important is what a slow-growing economy means for the American people, who increasingly feel trapped by their economic circumstances, with no way out. The threat to the American people has become existential. "If you shut Wall Street down, you won't have any industry," the senior Wall Street executive told me. "You won't have consumer loans. You won't have housing loans. You won't have fucking anything. Let's go back to the Middle Ages. Let's try it. You'll love the Middle Ages. It was great, if you forget bubonic plague, being drawn and quartered, and sort of living your entire life within around seven miles of where you were born. You'll love that shit. It's great, the Middle Ages."

ACKNOWLEDGMENTS

First and foremost, I would like to thank Joy Harris, my extraordinary and wise agent, for encouraging me to write this book after a conversation we had about the mysteries of Wall Street and why it had become the focus of so much public and political anger in the years after the 2008 financial crisis. She has been steadfast in her support since I became a writer in 2004. I cannot thank her enough.

I also want to thank especially David and Linda Supino, my longtime friends and colleagues from my years at Lazard, who graciously and selflessly took the time to read the manuscript and made many helpful suggestions for ways to improve it. I have incorporated their invaluable insights. They had much more productive ways to spend their time than reading through my pages, and I appreciate greatly that they did.

To Ben Greenberg, my editor at Random House, I will forever be grateful for your enthusiastic support in wanting this book to be written in the first place, for your editorial judgment along the way, and for your hard work in bringing it to fruition in a short period of time. You have been masterful. I also want to thank Caitlin McKenna, another editor at Random House, who read the manuscript carefully at Ben's request and raised many important questions and clarifications. Also, at Random House, I want to thank Gina Centrello, Susan Kamil, and Andy Ward, who from the start also shared Ben's enthusiasm for the project, as well as Benjamin Dreyer, Barbara Fillon, Andrea DeWerd, and Melanie DeNardo.

As ever, it takes a village to write a book. And so I want to again thank those friends who have provided me with invaluable support along the way, including Peter Davidson and Drew McGhee (in the pole position), Benjamin Abramowitz, Suzanna Andrews, Diane Archer and Steven Presser, Charlie and Sue Bell, Clara Bingham and Joe Finnerty, Joan Bingham, Michael Brod, Mary and Brad Burnham, Bryan Burrough and Maggie Walsh, Jerome and M. D. Buttrick, John Buttrick and Alex Ching, Michael and Elizabeth Cannell, Alan and Pat Cantor, Graydon Carter, Sue Craig, Don and Anne Edwards, John and

ACKNOWLEDGMENTS

Tracy Flannery, Tom Flexner, Al Garner, Jessica and Drew Guff, Stu and Barbara Jones, Fran and Michael Kates, Jon Kelly, Jamie Kempner, Peter Lattman and Isabel Gillies, Jeffrey Leeds and Elizabeth Marshall, Tom and Amanda Lister, Jane Mayer and William Hamilton, Bethany McLean, Joan McPhee and Michael Gilson, Esther Newberg, Eric Osserman, Jay and Massa Pelofsky, Richard Plepler, Adam Reed, David Resnick and Cathy Klema, Eileen Rudden and Josh Posner, Andy and Courtney Savin, Charlie Schueler, Pam Scott and Phil Balshi, Gil Sewall, Robert and Francine Shanfield, Jim and Sue Simpson, Andrew Ross Sorkin, Peter Soros and Electra Toub, Eliot Spitzer, Jeff and Kerry Strong, Doug Stumpf, Cyrus and Peggy Vance, William Van Deventer, Helmut and Caroline Weymar, Kit White and Andrea Barnet, Jay and Louisa Winthrop, Dan Yergin and Angela Stent, Tim and Nina Zagat, and, of course, Gemma Nyack. Thanks, too, are due my dear friends and colleagues at *Vanity Fair, The New York Times, Fortune,* CNN, and Bloomberg TV for their ongoing support.

I also want to thank, for putting up with me generally, my in-laws and relatives, the Futters, the Shutkins, the Hiekens, the Feldmans, and the rest of the extended Cohan clan. My parents, Sue and Paul, and my brothers, Peter and Jamie, are the best anyone could ever hope for. As for my wife of twenty-five years, Deb Futter, and my two incomparable sons, Teddy and Quentin, what can I say that hasn't already been said other than I love you very, very much.

I am hopeful that *Why Wall Street Matters* will help us to turn the page on the 2008 financial crisis and to get on with the important business of returning a reformed Wall Street to the central role it must play in keeping our economy humming. Obviously, any errors in fact, of omission, or of commission are my responsibility alone.

BIBLIOGRAPHY

Buck, James E. *The New York Stock Exchange: The First 200 Years*. Essex, Conn.: Greenwich, 1992.

Chernow, Ron. *Alexander Hamilton*. New York: Penguin Press, 2004.

Clews, Henry. *Twenty-Eight Years in Wall Street*. New York: Irving, 1887.

Galbraith, John Kenneth. *The Great Crash 1929*. Boston: Houghton Mifflin, 1955.

Hill, Frederick Trevor. *The Story of a Street: A Narrative History of Wall Street from 1644 to 1908*. New York: Harper, 1908.

Kindleberger, Charles P., and Robert Z. Aliber. *Manias, Panics, and Crashes: A History of Financial Crises*. Hoboken, N.J.: John Wiley & Sons, 2005.

BIBLIOGRAPHY

Mackay, Charles. *Extraordinary Popular Delusions*. New York: Dover, 2003.

Rothbard, Murray N. *The Panic of 1819: Reactions and Policies*. New York: Columbia University Press, 1962.

Shorto, Russell. *The Island at the Center of the World: The Epic Story of Dutch Manhattan and the Forgotten Colony That Shaped America*. New York: Vintage Books, 2005.

Strouse, Jean. *Morgan: American Financier*. New York: Random House, 1999.

ABOUT THE AUTHOR

WILLIAM D. COHAN, a former senior Wall Street M&A investment banker for seventeen years at GE Capital, Lazard Frères & Co., Merrill Lynch, and JPMorgan Chase, is the *New York Times* bestselling author of three nonfiction narratives about Wall Street: *Money and Power: How Goldman Sachs Came to Rule the World; House of Cards: A Tale of Hubris and Wretched Excess on Wall Street*; and *The Last Tycoons: The Secret History of Lazard Frères & Co.*; and the winner of the 2007 Financial Times and Goldman Sachs Business Book of the Year Award. He is also the author of the *New York Times* bestseller *The Price of Silence: The Duke Lacrosse Scandal, the Power of the Elite, and the Corruption of Our Great Universities*. He is a special correspondent at *Vanity Fair* and writes a biweekly opinion column for the DealBook section of *The New York Times*. He also writes for publications including the *Financial Times, Bloomberg Businessweek, The Atlantic, Fortune,* and *The Nation*. He is a graduate of Phillips Academy (Andover), Duke University, the Columbia University School of Journalism, and the Columbia University Graduate School of Business.

williamcohan.com
@WilliamCohan

ABOUT THE TYPE

The text of this book was set in Filosofia, a typeface designed in 1996 by Zuzana Licko, who created it for digital typesetting as an interpretation of the eighteenth-century typeface Bodoni, designed by Giambattista Bodoni (1740–1813). Filosofia, an example of Licko's unusual font designs, has classical proportions with a strong vertical feeling, softened by rounded droplike serifs. She has designed many typefaces and is the cofounder of *Emigre* magazine, where many of them first appeared. Born in Bratislava, Czechoslovakia, in 1961, Licko came to the United States in 1968. She studied graphic communications at the University of California, Berkeley, graduating in 1984.

DATE DUE

**This item is Due on
or before Date shown.**

MAR − − 2017